What Every Man Should Know about the "New Woman"

What Every Man Should Know about the "New Woman"

A Survival Guide

Steve Carter

McGraw-Hill Book Company

New York St. Louis San Francisco Bogotá Guatemala
Hamburg Lisbon Madrid Mexico Montreal Panama
Paris San Juan São Paulo Tokyo Toronto

1 2 3 4 5 6 7 8 9 0 F G R F G R 8 7 6 5 4

ISBN 0-07-010163-9

LIBRARY OF CONGRESS CATALOGING IN PUBLICATION DATA

Carter, Steve, 1956–
What every man should know about the new woman.
1. Women—Psychology. 2. Dating (Social customs)
3. Women—Sexual behavior. 4. Men—Sexual behavior.
5. Interpersonal relations. I. Title
HQ1206.C275 1984 646.7'7 83-25616
ISBN 0-07-010163-9 (pbk.)

Book design by Nancy Dale Muldoon

For Elaine

Contents

Acknowledgments

FIRST, my sincerest thanks to my agent, Julia Coopersmith, without whom none of this would have been possible, and to my editors PJ Haduch and Ken Stuart, whose creative input and guidance are greatly appreciated.

I also wish to express my appreciation to the countless numbers of men and women I have interviewed, and to my many friends who have helped me with this project, with special thanks to: Vince Cali, Frank Ettus, Marilyn and John Whitney, Grace Freedson, Josh Levine, Matt Rennert, Lee and Dick Kirstein, Jules Leventhal, Kenny Lindner, Steve Shukow, Nancy Jackson, Ruth and Bob Livingston, Bill Hurowitz, Terry Ryan, Reggie Ryan, and of course, Jorge.

In addition, my thanks to my family, with a special

thank-you to my brother-in-law Michael, who saved me from spending my entire advance on legal fees.

Last, but far from least, I wish to thank Elaine, to whom this book is dedicated, for her invaluable inspiration, encouragement, understanding, and patience.

What Every Man Should Know about the "New Woman"

INTRODUCTION

The Myth of the "Perfect Catch"

EVERYONE used to tell me that I was a "perfect catch." Foolishly,I believed them. After all, I was sensitive, understanding, personable,and most of all, I had a promising career in medicine ahead of me. What more could a woman want? But after going through a series of short-lived disasters which could barely be called relationships, I slowly began to realize that my perfect catch status was not all it was cracked up to be.

Baffled by my social failures, I turned to my friends for counsel. But they were experiencing similar problems, and their advice was tainted by their own bitterness. In fact, the more I spoke with my friends, the more obvious it became that none of us had the slightest idea as to what today's woman really wanted from a man.

It is quite conceivable that the answers to my social dilemma could have eluded me eternally. But through a strange twist of fate, it proved to be only a short time before these answers were well within my grasp.

It all started falling into place when, for reasons too complicated to discuss here, I shed my doctor's whites, donned my tennis whites, and headed for the Caribbean to become the Director of Tennis at a well-known island resort. Although this lifestyle was not always as glamorous as it sounds, it did provide me with one very important thing: an endless stream of stories about people's personal lives—stories which included explicit details of their romance problems, sexual problems, and more. It seems that these people naturally assumed that since I was a tennis pro, I had to be far more "experienced" than they were, and more capable of giving good advice.

At first, I just listened to these stories, trying to offer as little tangible guidance as possible since I was usually just as confused by their problems as they were. But as time passed, stories began to repeat themselves—the particulars were, of course, always different, but the underlying patterns were remarkably alike. What was even more fascinating to me was that some of these patterns closely resembled those that my past social failures had followed.

As I grew more interested in the information people were sharing with me, I began recording what I had heard, and in less than a year I had collected four full notebooks of stories, opinions, questions, and complaints. Shortly thereafter, I started conducting structured interviews with any willing male or female subjects, using questions that probed deeper and deeper into the heart of the trouble between the sexes. Finally, using all of the information I had accumulated, I carefully synthesized an accurate picture of the problems men face in their relationships with the "new woman," as well as a means to overcome these problems. At last I really *was* capable of giving troubled men the advice they so desperately needed.

In the Fall of 1982, I returned to New York to share this advice in a series of seminars entitled, "FOR MEN ONLY: Sex, Relationships, and the 'New Woman,' " which I taught through one of New York City's largest adult education networks: The Learning Annex. My experiences teaching these seminars strongly reinforced what I had learned over the years in the Caribbean, and provided the finishing touches for this book.

I hope the information which follows is as enlightening for you to read as it was for me to gather.

Steven A. Carter
New York, N.Y.

1

The "New Woman": Business before Pleasure?

SOMETHING IS WRONG. Dating is no longer enjoyable . . . the pressure to perform is taking the joy out of sex . . . fear of rejection is immobilizing us all. If you're sensitive, women think you're weak. Try to act stronger, they say you're too macho. Even if you defy the odds, and some semblance of a relationship manages to materialize, it is usually short-lived. What is it with women today? What do they want?

Men have always been perplexed by the female of the species. It is written that even the great Sigmund Freud, after years of research, finally threw his hands in the air and cried, "What do women want?" Perhaps it is somewhat comforting to know that a genius such as Freud was sometimes just as confused as the rest of us. But even Freud, were he alive,would be forced to admit that today's male faces the greatest challenge ever. This is because fast-paced changes in the last two decades have shattered age-old patterns of social and sexual interaction. The hard and fast rules are gone; time-tested strategies no longer work. Even when we try to learn from our mistakes, we gain little insight into the problem. Continuing to evaluate our failures using beliefs and attitudes which are no longer valid, we always come to the same conclusion: we didn't do anything wrong—something or someone else must be at fault.

Some of us have held "chemistry" accountable for our troubles, insisting that the woman wasn't really our type, or vice versa. While I will not deny that some relationships were never meant to be, the dynamics of male/female interaction go way beyond simple chemistry. If not, how could one explain why the relationships that *have* so much potential—those that could work, or should work—often fail to work? Surely you can't say that the chemistry just disappears—something has to *make* it disappear. It is this "something" which many of us make the mistake of overlooking.

Those of us who do not blame chemistry often make the more serious mistake of letting the blame fall on a far more obvious target: women. We convince ourselves that women just use men—that they are insensitive, manipulative, and two-faced. These excuses may help ease the pain, but the relief is, at best, temporary. As soon as we try again—playing the masculine role the only way we know how—more rejections follow. Bitter and disillusioned, we rant on and on about how horrible women are. But things fail to improve.

As long as we continue to approach our relationships using the same old attitudes and behavior patterns, our problems will not be solved. Women are not the selfish, unemotional, castrating sex-machines that many bitter men would have us believe, and it is time we stopped blaming them or bad chemistry for all of our troubles. Instead, we must open ourselves to a new style of social interaction that will enable us to have positive, rewarding relationships in the 1980's.

The search for a more successful method of social interaction begins by taking a closer look at the new woman. What does she want? What does she need? What turns her on? What turns her off? The answers to these questions will help us reeducate ourselves, and will enable us to develop the confidence and ability to complement this new breed of woman.

The Rush Is Over

When vast numbers of women started entering the work force a few decades ago, many men were probably laughing quietly to themselves—now women could finally experience firsthand all of the pressure and aggravation that was a way of life for so many men.

But a surprising thing happened. Women found their careers to be not only a way of obtaining self-sufficiency and security, but also a source of tremendous self-satisfaction and ego gratification. With this discovery, a woman's work immediately became more than just a means of obtaining security and independence, it became an end in itself—a vital component of the self-actualization process.

Today, as an ever-increasing number of women discover the fulfillment of a career, fewer women remain dedicated to the single-minded quest for marriage, home, and family. But as the relative importance of these once-popular pursuits steadily declines, our importance seems to diminish accordingly. Suddenly we are finding ourselves sharing center stage with other needs and interests which have become increasingly more meaningful to women; it is hard not to notice that women are devoting more and more time to these interests, and less and less time to us.

Does this mean that women have become more interested in making it in business than in making it with men? Well, women are certainly dedicated to developing their careers, and for good reason: common sense should tell us that a promising career is far more rewarding than a bad relationship. But women are not any more or any less dedicated to their work than men have always been to theirs. And just as men continue to recognize the importance of having relationships as well as careers,so do women.

However, women's new feelings of self-sufficiency and self-esteem *have* put the relationship in a new perspective, giving them a very different attitude toward choosing a man as a potential friend, lover, or spouse. What are these women now looking for? Where do intimate relationships fit into their new lifestyles? Women's answers to these questions reveal that first and foremost:

> Most women are no longer in any rush to get involved in a serious relationship, and they do not want to be pressured into doing so.

With women's new sense of independence and self-confidence putting an end to their dependency on men, the frantic search for male companionship has also ended. They no longer feel pressured to settle down with the first half-decent prospect that comes along, but instead, feel free to take their time, experiment with their emotions (and sometimes, ours), and look for more than just a meal ticket. As one woman commented to me, "We can afford not to be desperate."

If this were the only change to have taken place in women's attitudes, most men could easily accept it and learn to adjust. After all, no man really wants a woman whose interest in him is based solely on desperate economic need. But other, more complicated changes have taken place as well. More than ever before, women are willing to devote the vast majority of their time and energy to their careers, even if it means having to postpone the fulfillment of other needs such as marriage and family.

Fran L., an account executive in a New York advertising firm, explained it like this: "Nobody really worries about being labeled an old maid anymore. The phrase is an anachronism. None of my friends want to get married right now . . . some don't want to get married at all. What we *do* want is to get our careers in order." Is this point of view unique? Quite the contrary—it typifies the feelings of a sizeable percentage of the female population. Although women are very comfortable with this new attitude, it spells trouble for men with a more traditional point of view—namely, men who are not willing to wait as long as women to fulfill all of their needs.

This new attitude is creating another problem for today's male, for the longer a woman remains single, the more likely she is to resist getting involved in a serious relationship in the future. Anne M., a successful photojournalist from Connecticut, explains: "Once you have worked long and hard to establish a comfortable lifestyle for yourself, you're in no rush to give it up for some guy you hardly know, regardless of how terrific he seems to be."

But men's troubles do not end here, for most women are not just "in no rush" to get involved, they have become hypersensitive to, and are running away from, any man who pressures them into getting involved too quickly, regardless of whether or not he is doing it intentionally. But why is this such a serious problem? Because whether or not you realize it, every single aspect of male/female social interaction puts pressure on women.

Think about it. A large portion of the singles' scene revolves around superficial, high-pressured meeting environments like singles' bars (while alternatives can be just as uncomfortable). Sex and dating, once two clearly distinct phenomena, have become hopelessly intertwined, making dating a high-pressured, often unpleasant experience. Even the course of a relationship is not allowed to proceed at its natural pace, but instead, is forced forward by possessive men who need to be able to claim women as their property.

Not a pleasant picture, is it? Truthfully, there is almost nothing about our currently practiced patterns of social interaction that has remained relaxed, natural, or spontaneous. One woman clearly pointed this out when she complained to me: "You've barely learned a guy's first name before you're pressured to decide whether or not you want to go out with him, sleep with him, marry him . . . it's insane!"

It *is* insane, especially when you look at it from a woman's point of view. Unlike men, who are notorious for falling in love at first sight (especially when they have "sighted" a pronounced bustline or shapely behind), women are not so quick to form such strong attachments. Superficial characteristics rarely work the same magic on a woman as they work on a man, and for a woman to develop a sincere emotional interest in a man, she needs to go beyond these characteristics and find out what, if anything, lies underneath. But this process takes time—*lots of time*—and women have run out of patience for men who won't let a relationship proceed at its natural pace.

Men, unfortunately, are not sensitive to this. They seem to be unable to understand (or they choose to ignore) the fundamental differences between the male and the female emotional development processes, and naively assume that if they immediately feel a certain way about a woman, she should feel the same way about them just as quickly. Although, given a sufficient amount of time, the woman *could* feel this way, without ample time, she will not. This results in a disparity which can easily ruin a relationship before it has had any chance to develop.

Why do men get so carried away? Some men claim they cannot control themselves; they insist that falling in love makes it impossible to adhere to the rules of logic and reason. Other men are genuinely convinced that this type of behavior will ultimately win over a woman's heart, regardless of how negative her initial reaction may be. This idealized view of relationships is given ample support by Hollywood movie magic and other happily-ever-after media products.

In real life, unfortunately, our scenes don't always have such happy endings. For example, I recently spoke with a man who had been devastated by a bad experience with a woman with whom he had "fallen helplessly in love." This man, Jim, told me he had always thought of himself as a confirmed bachelor, committed to juggling at least two or three different relationships simultaneously. He had even developed somewhat of a reputation for this where he lived, and was proud of it. He also said he had been very content with this lifestyle, and expected to continue on in this fashion for some time to come. "I thought I had the best of all possible worlds," he admitted.

But one day it happened. A friend introduced him to a woman who was completing her law degree at a nearby university. By the end of his first date, he had gone absolutely nuts over her. Suddenly, everything looked very different to him; the bachelor's lifestyle had lost all of its appeal overnight.

The first thing Jim did was to call up the three women he had been dating at the time. He informed each one that he would not be seeing them anymore because he had "met someone very special." Next, he called up the law student to tell her how and why he had just broken off all of his other relationships. He expected her to find this incredibly romantic, but as you may already suspect, the woman was not moved by his gesture (or, perhaps more accurately, she was not moved in the right direction). The next time he called to ask her out, she told him she had too much studying to do. When he called her again, her excuse was flimsier. The third time he called, she said she didn't think they should see each other again. He was devastated—he couldn't understand what he had done wrong.

I explained to Jim that Ms. Right's sudden loss of interest was very predictable—most women would have had a similar reaction given those circumstances. The exact reason varies from woman to woman, but it usually follows one of the following lines of reasoning:

- The woman may have thought, "I'm just not ready for anything this serious—after all, I hardly know this guy." A woman can have this type of reaction even if she really likes you. It's not *you* that is turning her off, it is the *pressure* you're putting on her.

• The woman may have quickly decided, "I don't feel the same way about him—I'd better end this fast." In this instance, the woman has been turned off before she has ever had the chance to be turned on. Again, this doesn't mean that the woman didn't like you, it just means that she didn't like you *enough* to want to get involved in something which you were already taking far too seriously. (Given more time, she could have had a very different reaction.)

• The woman may have wondered, "How could he feel this way about me? He has only known me for one hour and fourteen minutes. For all he knows, I could be on the F.B.I.'s ten most-wanted list." In this case, the superficial basis of your infatuation has turned the woman off. Many women, being much more level-headed when it comes to forming their attractions, have:

1. No sympathy for men who are prone to falling in love too quickly—especially since these men tend to fall out of love just as quickly.
2. No tolerance for men who appear to be led around by their libido.

What is particularly unfortunate about this story, and the many stories like it, is that it didn't have to have such an unpleasant ending. If Jim hadn't said or done anything so drastic—if he had just given the woman some time to get to know him better without making her feel pressured or rushed—she could easily have developed an equal, or stronger, emotional attraction to him. But he never gave her the chance. In fact, most men never give women the chance.

But how *do* you give a woman the chance?

Must Men Play Hard-to-Get?

One evening, while eating dinner in my favorite Chinese restaurant, I found the following message inside my fortune cookie: "A woman is like your shadow. Follow her, she flies. Fly, she follows." For a moment, this made me wonder whether or not Confucius (or whoever wrote this little gem) was right.

There is no denying that it is human nature to place great value on what we must work hard to obtain, and take for granted that which falls into our laps too easily, even if it is a relationship. There is also no denying that a woman is going to be turned off by a man whose actions make her feel that he is begging her to get involved in a relationship. As I will discuss in detail shortly, women are looking for a man they can respect, and a man who has to grovel clearly does not even have any self-respect.

In light of this, it should come as no surprise that the "Take me, I'm yours" approach has an unpleasantly high rate of failure, especially when the offer is made too soon. But does this mean that the only way to be successful with the new woman is to play games with her? Absolutely not. Women are not so much turned *on* by games, as they are turned *off* by pressure. In fact, games-playing can be a much bigger turn-off than excessive fawning. After all, by definition, in order to have a relationship, two people must relate, and any intelligent woman knows that it is impossible to relate very well to a man who maintains an aloof facade, no matter how attractive he may otherwise seem.

"But don't women play games?" you may well ask. It is important to clarify the answer to this often-asked question. The new woman isn't *playing* hard-to-get, she *is* hard to get, and it is going to take a lot more than infantile head-games to make her seriously interested in you. What *will* make her interested is a new approach to relationships—a happy medium that has neither the built-in turn-offs of the gamesmanship approach, nor the drawbacks of the doormat approach—an approach which is governed by the following three rules:

1. You must understand and accept that relationships don't develop according to any type of fixed schedule or plan, but that each grows at a different rate according to the personalities involved, the degree of initial attraction, and a variety of other factors particular to the two individuals involved and the circumstances surrounding them.

2. You must realize that any attempt to force this natural process forward—*i.e.*, *pressure*, in any way, shape, or form—will only hurt your chances for success.

3. You must learn to temper your behavior, so that it reflects your belief in rules 1 and 2. This means *you must learn to keep the pressure off*.

"BUT I NEVER PRESSURE WOMEN . . ."

If you are thinking to yourself, "But I never put any kind of pressure on women," stop and think again. I have already emphasized once that the very nature of our currently practiced patterns of social interaction make it inevitable that a woman feels pressured, whether or not you intend it or even realize it. In the following chapters, I will discuss this in far greater detail, and help you develop the viable alternative I have mentioned: a new approach which frees women from the many pressures they have grown to resent, and frees men from many pressures and problems as well. But for now, remember:

> The secret to beginning, developing, and maintaining positive, rewarding relationships with the new woman lies in keeping the pressure off!

2

Are You "Mr. Right"?

ALTHOUGH many women are no longer in any rush to get involved in a relationship, this does not mean that they wish to forever eliminate men from their lives. On the contrary, virtually all of the women I have interviewed made it very clear to me that they were looking forward to finding someone special to settle into a meaningful relationship with. But the word "special" disturbed me—I sensed it was a loaded qualifier.

Most of you probably understand my trepidations; as a result of bad experiences, we have all become convinced that women are searching for the male version of the perfect "10." Well, women *have* become very selective. They don't even try to deny it, but instead, openly admit they are comparing us and weighing the importance of our various attributes. In addition, many new priorities have appeared, often placing emphasis on qualities that were unimportant to a woman searching for a male provider. Suddenly we have a reason to worry. Will they think we are attractive? Smart? Interesting? Exciting?

Being compared is not a pleasant experience, but do we have any right to criticize? Haven't we always been notorious for our critical analyses of women, first scrutinizing their physical characteristics, then weighing other attributes if the first hurdle is passed? Our financial independence has always afforded us this luxury. We felt no pressure, so why settle for the first woman who came along? Why not do a little shopping? But now women are more secure. Doesn't it seem fair that they should also shop around? It certainly does, but even if you don't agree, you are still going to have to accept that women are no longer willing to settle for less than they feel they deserve.

Still, this is no reason to throw in the towel, for although women are shopping more, their shopping lists are not as unrealistic as we tend to think they are. In fact, the items on their lists are often far more reasonable than the items on ours.

Who Is "Mr. Wrong"?

What qualities does the new woman look for in "Mr. Right"? What qualities make her label a man "Mr. Wrong"? No two women are the same; each has a unique set of needs, and therefore, a unique idea of what kind of man can fulfill those needs. On the other hand, there *are* certain qualities which many or most women *tend* to look for, as well as certain qualities they *tend* to shy away from. It is necessary for you to become more aware of what these qualities are if you hope to get a better handle on your present and future relationships.

The following list of traits serves this purpose; they are traits most often mentioned by women when they are asked what it is they find most attractive and most unattractive in a man. It is important to note that this is *not* a list of "must be's" or "must not be's"—possession of any or all of the right traits does not guarantee success, nor does the lack of them guarantee failure. Therefore, do not use this list to help you decide whether or not you are a loser in the eyes of the new woman—this is not its purpose. What you should do is use this list for the reasons it was designed:

- To make you more aware of your most attractive qualities, and why you should make the most of them.
- To make you more aware of your least attractive qualities—qualities which may be hurting you—and why it may be worth the effort to try to change or eliminate them.
- To make you more aware of which qualities you may lack, and why it may be worth making a concerted effort to develop some of them.

With this in mind, let's now take a closer look at the qualities that are turning on and turning off the new woman:

SELF-CONFIDENCE

The quality you will find most often on women's lists of "turn-ons" is self-confidence. Self-confidence radiates in men who feel good about themselves and their lives, and this attracts women like a magnet. As you might expect, the flip side of this coin—excessive insecurity—is a big turn-off. It is hard for a woman to respect a man who doesn't respect himself, and a woman needs to respect the man she is involved with.

Of course it is easy for me to say that women are attracted to confident men, but how does someone build his confidence? I would be lying if I said this was simple, especially since lack of self-esteem tends to reinforce itself in a cycle that is difficult to break. Let me illustrate: a man evaluates himself and decides he does not possess the qualities women find most desirable. More often than not, this decision is based on a variety of mistaken assumptions. For example, he may think he's not handsome enough or rich enough. These qualities are relatively unimportant to a woman, but this man has been led to believe otherwise, and the result of his misevaluation is a very real and pronounced lack of self-esteem. When he interacts with women, his lack of confidence shows, and as a result, women are not attracted to him. This reinforces his feelings of inadequacy by virtue of a self-fulfilling prophecy.

How does someone break out of this no-win trap? It takes three steps:

1. *You must become aware of your positive qualities.*

Whenever I teach my "FOR MEN ONLY" seminar, I begin with a discussion of the traits the new woman looks for in a man (a discussion very similar to the one we are having right now). During one seminar, after going through my list of traits, I heard a man breathe a long sigh of relief. The class turned to look at him, and he blurted out, "I feel better already!" This was followed by a lot of nervous laughter from the other men in the class. Obviously, many of them knew exactly how he was feeling. They too had been harboring many misconceptions about the new woman—misconceptions which had been torturing their egos.

This man's reaction illustrates very clearly how a person's confidence can be boosted solely by the realization that he possesses many of the traits women find most attractive. This list will help you discover which ones you have (every man has some of them), and will help boost your ego too.

2. *You must use your best qualities to your advantage.*

Once you are aware of your best qualities, you must take full advantage of them, strengthen them if possible, and be sure not to hide them (if you've got it, flaunt it, so to speak). Nothing distresses me more than seeing a man who does not let his finest qualities show. For example, an acquaintance of mine possesses a marvelous sense of humor that is clearly one of his best qualities (I will discuss the importance of humor shortly). Ed's problem is that when he is with women, he takes on a completely different personality—so different, that if you were to ask one of his dates if she felt he was the funniest person she had ever met, she would probably think you were talking about someone else. This does not happen because Ed freezes up on dates, it happens because he is convinced that women are attracted to men who are suave, cool, and reserved, and not attracted to men who are loose, easy, and funny. Ed's misunderstanding has caused him to mask one of his most important assets. As you might expect, he has tremendous difficulty with most of his relationships, and lacks confidence because of this.

3. *You must make every effort to develop the qualities you feel you lack (if at all possible).*

Everyone has the potential to develop some, or all of the qualities on this list; all it takes is your willingness to work at it. Just remember that the results will justify the effort. Every small change you make will reinforce itself, helping to bring about a chain of events which will lead to more and more feelings of geniune self-esteem (a chain of events that proceeds in the exact opposite direction of the "no-win" trap I just discussed).

One word of warning: Although women are turned on by confident men, excessive confidence—*i.e.*, cockiness—is not at all attractive. Women detest an egomaniac who seems to have no place in his life for anyone but himself (especially since this threatens a woman's feelings of self-esteem), and women also tend to suspect that such gross overconfidence is a cover-up for a massive insecurity complex (which it usually is).

EXCESSIVE JEALOUSY AND/OR POSSESSIVENESS

High on women's lists of turn-offs are jealousy and possessiveness. There are two reasons for this:

1. Women interpret excessive jealousy and/or possessiveness as signs of insecurity. Remember, women are turned off by insecure men.

2. Women have struggled to establish a lifestyle for themselves in which they are free to pursue many things, including a career, avocational interests, friendships, and love relationships. It is *very* important for them to feel that they have the freedom to do as they wish, when they wish, including, if they so desire, the freedom to go out with more than one man. Therefore, it only makes sense that the very last thing these women want is a possessive, jealous male who comes along and immediately tries to put a big crimp in their lifestyle. Women do not want to be claimed as property, and they are immediately turned off by men who try to make such a claim—men who issue ultimatums, men who try to smother them, men who get insanely jealous, etc.

How do you rid yourself of the jealousy/possessiveness habit? It's not easy, but it can be done with the help of two things:

1. *Restraint*

Many times, your emotions will beg you to do one thing while logic urges you to do the opposite. During these difficult times (and believe me, I know how difficult they can be), you must keep your emotions under control by reminding yourself that it's one thing to expect certain concessions from a woman you've been seeing for a couple of years, but you can't expect anything from a woman you've been seeing for a couple of weeks (or even a couple of months). It may hurt like crazy at the time, but the long-term benefits far outweigh the short-term emotional costs.

2. *Confidence*

In many instances, a jealous or possessive reaction is completely unwarranted, but occurs because of a pronounced lack of confidence. It is time to start believing in yourself more. You have a lot to offer a woman—stop acting as though you don't (*i.e.*, by getting jealous over every other man who enters her life).

UNDERSTANDING AND SENSITIVITY

Few women fail to mention the importance of two perennial favorites: understanding and sensitivity. Today's woman wants a man who cares and communicates—not a man who is aloof and disinterested. She wants to be appreciated as an intellectually and emotionally complex human being, not as an object whose sole purpose is to attend to a man's sexual urges. Therefore, she is most attracted to a man who is emotionally receptive, a man who shows an interest in her as a person.

At this time, I would like to discuss a point which has been raised in several of my "FOR MEN ONLY" seminars. Every time I discuss the importance of emotional receptivity, the same objections are raised. "Women may *say* they want men who are understanding and sensitive," the men in my class tell me, "but what they really want is something very different. Otherwise, we wouldn't be here." "I think sensitivity has been a detriment to my relationships," one man added, "not an aid." If you consider yourself to be a sensitive, understanding male, yet have found yourself with the short end of the stick in one too many relationships, you are probably nodding your head in agreement.

Why does there seem to be such a contradiction? Why do women say they want sensitive, understanding men, only to turn around and give these same men the shaft a week or two later? Probably because there is a fine line between being sensitive, and *over*sensitive; between being understanding, and *too* understanding. In the past decade or two, there has been so much emphasis placed on the importance of emotional receptivity,that many men have crossed this line (unaware that this could actually hurt them). Once this happens, women are turned off—they view oversensitivity as a sign of insecurity, and they view excessive understanding as a sign of wimpiness. (As one woman said to me, "Every time I do something awful to him he says, 'I understand.' Just *once* I wish he said that he didn't understand—that he didn't understand one bit!")

Still, as I explain in my seminars, we must never dismiss the importance of openness and receptivity. Women really *do* want sensitive, understanding men; but they *also* want them to have a strong side. By placing too much emphasis on sensitivity and understanding, many of us have lost this strong side. It must be rebuilt; but as our emotional strength grows (and it will grow, through renewed confidence, a new attitude, and positive reinforcement), we must *never* lose touch with our ability to be emotionally receptive. Without this ability, we will not only lose our attractiveness to the opposite sex, but we will also deprive ourselves of some very healthy, rewarding experiences.

"MACHO-ITIS"

Several months ago, I sat in on a human sexuality class offered through one of New York City's adult education programs. At the end of the class, the instructor introduced me to everyone, and said a few words about the book I was writing. As I was leaving the class, an attractive woman who had been sitting near me stopped me at the door. "Do me a favor," she implored, "will you please tell those men that 'macho' is finished . . . dead . . . over!" Her request did not shock me at all—I expect that many women would ask a similar favor, given the opportunity. I am honoring this woman's request, and passing this on to you here in her exact words for a very good reason: She is right—macho *is* finished. In fact, in a recent nationwide survey, women rated macho attitudes as the number-one turn-off. This is particularly interesting when you consider that so many men are convinced that macho attitudes are the number-one aphrodisiac. Clearly, there is a breakdown in communication between the sexes.

Why do women loathe macho attitudes? Because these attitudes are the antithesis of what the new woman is all about. As Allison R., a lawyer from Chicago, clearly explained, "Macho men show no respect for women as intelligent human beings—their attitude is simply 'woman as bitch,' 'woman as sex object to be conquered and discarded.' It's disgusting." This is not to say that the new woman wants to be treated like one of the guys; she doesn't. But anything is preferable to being treated like a piece of meat.

How does one cure himself of acute macho-itis? That depends on the nature of the infection. If, for example, you adopted a macho approach because you thought it would turn women on, all you have to do is dump this attitude and adopt a healthier one—one which focuses on the old saying, "Treat a woman the way you wish to be treated." If, on the other hand, your macho behavior is deeply imbedded in your personality (but you realize it is destroying your relationships), you may need to get some professional guidance if you are to kick the macho habit.

INDEPENDENCE

Today, women find themselves torn between the need for independence and the desire to involve themselves in a relationship. Some women are willing to sacrifice one for the other, but the vast majority are not. This is not to say that relationships are unimportant to these women, it is just that independence is equally, if not more important. In fact, many women believe that it is impossible to have a healthy, rewarding relationship if you cannot maintain your independence within that relationship. "A healthy relationship cannot exist if it is based on dependency," explained Joan B., a graduate student at Boston University, "for a relationship to thrive, mutual independence is vital."

The new woman is looking for a man who can offer her the best of both worlds: a man who is capable of having a relationship, while simultaneously respecting a woman's need for her independence. What kind of a man is capable of doing this? A man who values his own independence. As Ellen L., a West Coast CPA, remarked, "What do I want? A man who respects my independence, and respects his own. He must do *both*. If he is threatened by my independence, the relationship will fail." Emily S., a paralegal from California, explained her independence needs in somewhat less abstract terms, "I don't want to have to lean on a man all of the time, and I don't want a man who is always leaning on me. Any man who makes me feel obligated to spend every waking moment with him, obligated to include him in all my plans, and obligated to explain why when I don't, won't last a week with me. I can't respect a guy like that."

INTELLIGENT/ INTERESTING

"I like interesting men," Jane B., a very successful dress designer once told me, "men with interesting jobs, interesting hobbies, interesting information, interesting opinions. . . . Men should stop spending so much time expanding their biceps, and start expanding their minds." This woman's point is well made. Far too many men waste their time trying to develop superficial characteristics which they *think* will attract a woman (everyone knows those enlarging devices don't work anyway). Instead, men should be putting their time to better use, developing the one part of their anatomy that really does turn a woman on: their brains.

Of course, when women talk about the importance of intelligence, they don't mean they are searching for a man who scored over 1400 on his college boards. Intelligence, to a woman, is an ability to communicate; a willingness to exchange ideas and share opinions, and to understand the importance and implications of this information. In other words, women aren't looking for a man with three Ph.D.'s, they're looking for the guy who scores highest in human relations.

AMBITIOUSNESS

The new woman has rebelled against a history of financial dependency, and she is proud of her accomplishments. Out in the business world, working hard to support herself, it has become difficult for her to respect a man who isn't doing the same thing (in the 60's, the opposite was true, but all that has changed), and the last thing today's woman wants is to find herself supporting a lazy, unambitious man.

It is important to understand that it is not money, nor money-making potential that attracts a woman to an ambitious man—the new woman has her own money—it is his attitude about his work that women find so attractive. Sound hard to believe? Then you should be interested to learn that during the course of my interviewing, only about 10 percent of the women said that the amount of money a man had, or was capable of making, was an important criterion in their search for "Mr. Right." Most women, on the other hand, were adamantly opposed to this, stressing that they were proud of their financial self-sufficiency, and had fought hard to liberate themselves from the search for a meal ticket.

DEPTH

Women love men with depth; men who can talk to them—really talk. "There is nothing that turns me off more than a man who can only make small talk," said Bonnie G., a dancer from New York City. "You know what I mean? A guy who talks about his clothes, his apartment, his car . . . but never about *himself.*" I hear this stressed often by all types of women, and by now you shouldn't be surprised to be reading it here. After all, if understanding, sensitivity, and intelligence are at the top of women's most-wanted lists, it only makes sense to find superficiality at the top of their least-wanted lists.

If you have a serious side, don't be afraid to show it—it's what most women are looking for in a man.

SENSE OF HUMOR

What surprised me the most during my interviews was the frequency with which women mentioned the importance of sense of humor. In fact, it was mentioned almost as often as many of the far more "serious" qualities. Why? Because sense of humor reflects far more than a man's ability to say or appreciate something funny—it is a reflection of his personality, his intelligence, his self-confidence, his sensitivity . . . his entire attitude toward himself and his life. Humorlessness, on the other hand, is indicative of much more than a boring personality—it can reflect tremendous insecurity, depression, a controlled, manipulative personality, or other undesirable traits. Therefore, don't be afraid to let your sense of humor show—women want to see it.

I should issue one word of caution. A sense of humor is very important, but it is also important for a man to be able to show that he has a serious side. The chronic clown or jokester may be entertaining (at least, for a while), but women find it difficult to develop a serious attraction to this type of man.

PHYSICAL APPEARANCE

What about looks? Men will be most interested to learn what women have to say about the importance of physical appearance. More than three-quarters of the women I interviewed said that a man's looks were not very important. Surprised? Probably because men place a much higher premium on looks than women do. (If I were to ask men about their preferences, I suspect that at least half would say that a woman's looks were very important to them.)

Again, we see the classic split between the sexes. On the one hand, we have men responding to superficial characteristics; on the other, we have women looking for more meaningful qualities. I cannot refrain from pointing out that men could learn a lesson here from the opposite sex.

There are two other important lessons to be learned from this information.The first is for men who have a poor self-image because they think their looks turn women off. *It is not your looks that are turning women off—it is your bad self-image.* In other words, you are bringing on a self-fulfilling prophecy by letting your feelings about your looks affect your overall feelings about yourself. It is time to stop feeling sorry for yourself because you don't look like Tom Selleck, and realize that regardless of what you look like, many women will be attracted to you if you feel good about yourself.

The second lesson is for men who spend most of their time and money working on their physical appearance. When it comes to choosing between looks, and less superficial characteristics (intelligence, understanding, etc.), the latter is a hands-down favorite every time. Even the best-looking men in the world won't be able to hold on to a woman if they can't fulfill her emotional needs. Therefore, as I said earlier, start developing things which are more important than your left bicep (and I don't mean your right bicep!).

Before I end this discussion, I must point out that there is one instance where physical appearances play a somewhat more important role: when you're meeting someone for the first time. Still, there is no reason to be overly concerned, for even in this instance, you don't have to look like Paul Newman, or be built like Arnold Schwarzenegger to make a good impression—you just have to be well-groomed.

Women are turned off by sloppy men, so if you're trying to make a good impression, it would help to get yourself a good haircut, give yourself a clean shave, tuck in your shirt (take it off if it's an old T-shirt), put on a decent pair of pants (the ones that aren't air-conditioned), and leave your ratty sneakers in your closet. Your neat appearance will get you past those critical first few minutes, and after that, women will be far more concerned with finding out what kind of a person you are (again, it is only men who remain hung up on looks for any length of time).

Though not mentioned as often as the items listed above, there are several other very important qualities that many women discussed during their interviews. The positive qualities include: warmth, kindness, a positive mental attitude (a so-called "up" person), and sincerity. The negative qualities include: insincerity, excessive aloofness, and a negative mental attitude. Be sure to make a note of these traits—they can have as significant an effect on your relationships as any of the other qualities discussed above.

A Winning Combination

What kind of man is the new woman looking for? If I had to sum up all of the answers I've heard in one sentence, I would say this:

> Women want a man they can respect, and a man who respects them in turn—a strong, confident man who possesses a sensitive side.

This explains why women are turned on by traits which reflect emotional strength *and* emotional receptivity. It also explains why women are turned off by traits which show excessive weakness and/or lack of receptivity—traits such as insecurity, possessiveness, and macho attitudes.

You may point out that the type of man the new woman is looking for doesn't seem to be very different from the type of man women have always looked for. This may be true, but do not forget that there are two fundamental differences between the attitudes of the "new woman" and those of the traditional woman:

- While traditionally, women may have been happy to find a man who possessed *a few* of the positive qualities we've discussed, today, women may not be willing to get seriously involved with a man who does not possess *most, if not all* of the qualities she desires (assuming, of course, that her expectations are realistic).
- Unlike the highly tolerant woman-of-the-past, the new woman is apt to walk away from any man who pressures her to get involved in a relationship before she is good and ready. This holds true regardless of how many positive qualities the man possesses.

Now that you have a better understanding of women's new attitudes, you are almost ready to begin developing a new approach to your relationships with these women. But first, it is necessary to examine one more important aspect of the modern relationship: sex.

3

Sexual Fallout: Aftermath of the Revolution

EVER since it began, the sexual revolution has been a subject of social controversy. At first, everyone welcomed it with open arms, hailing it as the end of an oppressive taboo—an opportunity to express strong physical and emotional desires in the absence of guilt or social disapproval. But what has this great liberation really brought? In the minds of many men, the sexual revolution has created far more problems than it has solved, largely because it has encouraged the development of what these men see as a twentieth-century monster: the sexually experienced single woman.

Today's women, having accumulated an unprecedented amount of sexual experience and expertise, appear to be wreaking havoc upon the male population, leaving an unending number of psychologically traumatized men in their wake. By the tender age of fifteen, girls are already reading the sexual advice columns in *Cosmopolitan* with 100 percent comprehension (while their naive parents attempt to explain to them the difference between little girls and little boys); by the time they are twenty, the vast majority have long since abandoned their virgin status. What does this mean for young men looking forward to sexual intimacy? Will they be forced to face partners already preoccupied with having multiple orgasms?

The scenario is frightening, and it gets even worse as we grow older. Every time a man gets into a woman's bed, he knows others have probably been there before him. For some of us, this has come to mean terror. We are haunted by ghosts of our partner's previous lovers. Instead of joy and pleasure, there is only the fear of evaluation and comparison. Do we measure up? Were we as good as the last one? Pressured into proving our masculinity, obsessed with "doing it" better than the others, and fearing failure, we place exaggerated emphasis on sexual skills. Bedroom conversations focus on the female orgasm and performance evaluation; the tender pillow talk is gone.

Shifting our attention from sexual intimacy to sexual performance, we have taken the warmth out of the bedroom, leaving behind an emotional void—an environment in which our masculinity is constantly being put to the test. This is having a terribly negative effect on our attitudes toward women, toward ourselves, and toward our sexuality.

If we are to come to terms with the sexual revolution and women's new attitudes toward sex and sexuality, we must first become more aware of what these new attitudes really are; many of us harbor gross misconceptions which are making our troubles far more traumatic than they need be. To help you develop this awareness, in this chapter I will address the many questions which are tormenting today's male—questions such as: How does today's woman view sex? Does she still think it's something special, or has it become nothing more than what a good-night kiss once was—an emotionless gesture of thanks for an evening of pleasant company? How many men has the average woman slept with, or are there too many to count? What about men's fears of being compared to women's previous lovers . . . do women really take a mental checklist with them to the bedroom? Women's honest answers to these and other important questions are enlightening, and are certain to affect the way you view women and the way you view yourself.

How Does the New Woman View Sex?

Not long ago, a man could take certain things for granted once he slept with a woman; but those days are gone. Now men don't know what to assume, or if they can assume anything at all. How *do* women feel about the men they sleep with? Of course, that depends on the woman, but my interviews have revealed four very interesting, and somewhat surprising attitudes which seem to be prevalent amongst today's women:

1. Sex is something most women still reserve for the privileged few.

2. Although sex is important, it is not necessarily a sign of love, commitment, or possession.

3. Many women find it difficult, if not impossible, to carry on simultaneous love affairs.

4. Women *are* evaluating their lover's performance.

It is in our best interests to carefully examine each of the above statements, one by one.

SEX FOR THE PRIVILEGED FEW

The sexual revolution has been so dramatically over-hyped that it is hard for anyone not to believe that the world has become one big sexual free-for-all. We are haunted by images of liberated women dragging every man they can get their hands on into their beds, and we prepare ourselves for every date accordingly (the "Toothbrush Syndrome"). Even the most perceptive, intelligent men have fallen victim to the media blitz—a fact I became aware of during a recent discussion with a group of university professors. After telling these men that I was preparing a book which examined the many problems men were having in their relationships with today's women, one professor remarked, "What kind of problems? I thought that these women can't wait to jump into bed with every man they meet. I wish I had those kinds of problems." The other professors laughed, and nodded their heads in agreement.

But the truth paints a very different picture of the new woman's sexual appetite. Although there is no denying that most women are having sex earlier, and maybe with greater frequency than they would have thirty years ago, today's women are *not* jumping into bed with every man they meet. Quite the contrary, sex has retained its importance to many women, and is regaining its importance to many others.

Sex has retained its importance. In spite of the sexual revolution, many women express little or no desire to have numerous sexual partners. For these women, sex always has been, and always will be something very special—a complex emotional and physical experience to be shared only with men they care about a great deal. The sexual revolution may have made it more comfortable for these women to sleep with a special partner once they find one, but it hasn't affected their attitude toward finding him. These women are just as selective as women were thirty years ago. Linda S., a thirty-five-year-old interior decorator from Maryland, remarked, "I've slept with very few men in my lifetime. For me, sex is too important to be practiced indiscriminantly. Sure, I may be somewhat more experienced than my mother was at my age, but I think that our attitudes toward sex are not very different—both of us recognize its importance, and the importance of sharing ourselves only with special men."

Sex is regaining its importance. Many other women were very much caught up in the sexual revolution. But experimentation with their new freedom proved to be extremely disappointing as they discovered that sex without emotional involvement tended to be an empty, and often depressing experience. In fact, a famous study of women's attitudes toward sex, published as *The Cosmo Report,** revealed that *over 50 percent* of the more than 100,000 *Cosmopolitan* magazine readers surveyed spoke negatively of the sexual revolution. Of this 50 percent, two thirds specifically complained that the sexual revolution had "caused sex to be too casual,"and that they felt, "sex should be saved for a 'meaningful' relationship." The other one third complained "the sexual revolution made it hard for [them] to find acceptable reasons to say no to a man sexually." Many women have expressed similar feelings to me, some going so far as to accuse men of creating the sexual revolution in order to have a better excuse to pressure women into bed.

But whatever, or whomever, is responsible for the sexual revolution is unimportant; what *is* important is that a counterrevolution has begun. Women (as well as many men) are turning away from mindless promiscuity and rejecting the concept of sex as sport, in an effort to put much-needed meaning back into their relationships. Everywhere we look, catch-phrases such as "Is sex dead?" or "The New Celibacy" are appearing, signaling that the sexual revolution has certainly passed out of its prime, and may even be heading for an early grave which it has been digging for itself over the past twenty years.

* Wolfe, L., *The Cosmo Report*, New York: Arbor House, 1981.

* * *

Of course, there are women who still whole-heartedly embrace their sexual freedom, and boast of having partners too numerous to count. Yet though we read and hear about these women often, they represent a very small percentage. In fact, most current studies of women's sexual behavior patterns indicate that less than one sixth of the female population have had a substantial number of sexual partners (more than twenty) in their lifetimes (as opposed to almost two fifths of the male population). At the same time, some studies have revealed that *half* of the female population have had less than five or six sexual partners in their lifetimes (only one-fourth of the male population can make this claim), and this figure is likely to increase substantially in the next decade.

All of these statistics clearly demonstrate how important it is for men to understand that the new woman is not some kind of mindless nymphomaniac, but rather, a very sensible human being who holds a special place in her life for sexual intimacy. Indeed, if anyone is to be accused of mindless promiscuity, it is we, the male of the species.

Reviewing this information, it would make sense that the next question to ask is, "Who are the 'privileged few' that today's women choose to share their intimate moments with?"

The privileged few. Who do women sleep with? What kind of men do they find most sexually attractive? Men with expensive clothes? Bulging biceps? Massive genitals?

Although these are some of the answers men are likely to give, women's answers agree with "none of the above." Most women do not view sex as a brute physical act based solely on superficial physical attraction. Instead, they see it as a complex experience which results from a combination of strong emotional, intellectual, and physical attractions. Therefore, the qualities which turn a woman on reflect this complexity—they must turn her on emotionally and intellectually, as well as physically. What types of qualities elicit this reaction? The same ones I discussed in Chapter 2: qualities such as understanding, sensitivity, intelligence, and confidence.

A lot of men find this very difficult to understand, probably because the male sexual turn-on is often so different. When a man spots an attractive woman on the street, or even in a magazine, he may become instantly aroused, even though he knows absolutely nothing about the woman other than what she looks like. (Women tend to harshly criticize this type of reaction in men for its superficial nature, but all of this criticism may not be fair, since there is much evidence to suggest that men are all prisoners of a lifetime of cultural training and a highly sensitive hormonal network.) Women, on the other hand, are not as easily aroused by physical attributes, and rarely experience such an instantaneous sexual turn-on. If anything, their initial interest is more sensual than sexual, and even this can take time to surface.

It is important for you to be aware of the differences between these male and female trigger systems if you are to learn how to best encourage the development of a woman's sexual interest in you.

SEX IS IMPORTANT, BUT . . .

Even though women respect the importance of sexual intimacy and are selective about choosing their sexual partners, being picked as one of the "privileged few" does not entitle you to assume very much about the status of your relationship. Women are quick to point this out, insisting that men often take way too much for granted once they have started sleeping with someone. These women also point out that men's mistaken assumptions are often responsible for the rapid deterioration of their relationships. In order to understand this, let's take a closer look at some of the more important mistakes men tend to make when they sleep with a woman:

Mistaken Assumption #1: Sex indicates love. Although there are many men who have incorrectly concluded that women place no importance on sexual intimacy, there are also men who make the opposite error—they assume that any woman willing to sleep with them must also be madly in love with them. Though most women value the importance of sexual intimacy, and some *do* insist on love before sex, the *majority* of women *do not* consider love to be a necessary prerequisite for sex (not even for *good* sex). For these women, "like" has become as acceptable a premise for sex as love.

Men's inability to understand or accept this leads to two common pitfalls:

1. *The panic trap (Houdini Syndrome)*

"Men have a tendency to sleep with you once or twice, then disappear without a trace. They tell you that they'll call you in a few days, and you never hear from them again. Sometimes I wonder if they died or something . . . but deep down I know that they just panicked . . . freaked out . . . because they think they're in over their heads," said Ellen F., a lawyer from Chicago.

Many women have told me of their experiences with men who exhibit this Houdini-like behavior. These women all agree that the men grossly misinterpret women's feelings about sex, and this misunderstanding causes them to panic and run.

2. *The love trap*

"I don't understand it," one man complained to me. "We had been sleeping together for almost a week . . . I loved her . . . I thought she loved me. . . ." I have heard this a hundred times from a hundred different men. Too many of us use sexual intimacy as a convenient excuse to fall head-over-heels in love with a woman, naively assuming that the woman has done likewise. Two days later, when the woman announces that she has another date for that evening, we are devastated. We wonder to ourselves, "How could she have fallen out of love so quickly?" But the fact of the matter is that she was never *in* love to begin with.

As you can imagine, or perhaps are painfully aware of, this type of experience can shatter the male ego, and also generate a lot of anger toward the female of the species. This is not to say that you shouldn't fall in love with a woman, it is only to warn you not to *conveniently* fall in love with a woman (or fall in love with love) *only* because you think she has fallen in love with you.

The panic trap and the love trap seem to be complementary concepts, based upon the same misunderstanding. If you are under the mistaken assumption that any woman who sleeps with you is in love with you, it only makes sense that if you are unsure of your feelings toward her, you may panic, or that if you feel very strongly toward her, you may convince yourself that you too are in love. This implies that the man who burns women by vanishing after one night in her bed, is the same man who gets burned when he wakes up to discover that he loves a woman who does not love him. As you develop a clearer understanding of how women view sex, you will also develop more realistic expectations, and ultimately, hurt women less and hurt yourself less.

Mistaken Assumption #2: Sex indicates commitment. A friend of mine once called to tell me about the changes that had been taking place in his love life. He said he had recently been introduced to a terrific woman, and that the relationship was already, "in the bag." By using this expression, he was letting me know that he had been sleeping with her (many men love to brag about such things), and therefore, considered the relationship solidified. I tried to warn him that relationships are not solidified so easily, nor so quickly. But he just laughed and said, "You don't understand . . . it's in the bag!" Of course I "understood" far better than he did. I also understood when, a few weeks later, he called back to inform me that the woman of his dreams had turned around and "bagged" him. He was crushed, and of course, thoroughly mystified. "What did I do wrong?" he implored.

For one thing, he had taken way too much for granted. The women I have interviewed stress that just having sex is neither an indication of love, nor an indication of any type of commitment. This change in attitude is due to a change in the timing of our sexual behavior. Since sex enters many relationships fairly quickly, it no longer serves to culminate these relationships. Instead, it is seen as only one of the many important building blocks in a relationship. This means that *sex no longer functions as some sort of indestructible relationship glue*, and it is dangerous to assume otherwise. It certainly helps strengthen a relationship, but it alone is not enough to permanently bind one.

This has become increasingly evident as more and more women walk away from intimate sexual involvements—even if these are prolonged involvements. Their message is clear: *it takes a lot more than sex to make a relationship work—no relationship is ever "in the bag."*

Mistaken Assumption #3: Sex indicates ownership. Several months ago, one of the men in my seminar asked me if I could tell him why his relationships all followed the same depressing pattern. Three of the last four women he had gone out with had broken off the relationship less than three weeks after they started sleeping with him. He was beside himself. "Everything had been perfect," he insisted, "then . . . poof!"

I asked him a few questions in order to get a better grip on his situation. From our discussion, I concluded that sex itself didn't seem to be causing the problem. I, too, became puzzled, but then he said something that tipped me off. Two of the women had told him the exact same thing when they broke up with him: they said he, "needed too much." After more discussion, the man admitted to me that he could not accept a woman's need to be independent once she was involved with him. He expected his intimate companions to be constant companions, sharing all aspects of their lives with him at all times. This, he thought, was the way a couple should behave.

This man was burying himself over and over again because of the same mistaken assumption. No matter how many times you sleep with a woman—no matter how much she likes you or loves you—possessiveness is a turn-off. Sex is not an indication of possession, and sleeping with a woman once, twice, or even a thousand times does not entitle you to claim her as your property (at least not in this country). The new woman needs lots of room; she never wants to be smothered, nor feel obligated to spend every moment of her free time with someone—even if its someone she loves passionately. It chokes her independence and is not healthy for a relationship.

Now that you know what sexual intimacy does *not* indicate, it is only natural to ask what, if anything, *does* it indicate? If current trends continue, and I believe they will, it may not be very long before the vast majority of men and women once again view sex as an extremely significant statement of affection which is indicative of both love and commitment (it will never indicate possession). But for now, you must accept that a woman's desire to sleep with you may only indicate that your relationship has the *potential* to develop into something serious—a potential which can be realized through time and effort.

Therefore, if you are hoping to develop a meaningful relationship with a woman, the last thing you can afford to do is sit back and rest on your laurels just because you've slept with her a few times. Instead, you should be directing your energies toward helping the woman develop a stronger interest in you which could eventually lead to both love and commitment in the future.

TWO IS ONE TOO MANY

Many men have suffered from tremendous relationship anxiety ever since the sexual revolution picked up steam.

These men are constantly worried that the freedoms of the sexual revolution will tempt their partners to carry on several love affairs simultaneously (a temptation which men themselves often have difficulty resisting). This anxiety, if not checked, can lead to outright paranoia, as seen in the actions of suspicious men who constantly search for clues which will indicate that their lovers are cheating on them (a search reminiscent of women's classic search for lipstick on the collar of the unfaithful male).

This paranoid behavior can start a chain of events which, if not stopped, will end in disaster. For example, if a man is worried that his lover may be cheating on him, he becomes increasingly jealous, possessive, and distrustful. As these negative qualities surface, the woman becomes insulted and turned off by his insecurity and lack of trust. As this gets worse, she will find herself less and less attracted to him, and may start looking for someone else. When she finds someone new, her old lover will conclude that his suspicions were right—she really *was* cheating on him. But the sad truth is that she would have never looked elsewhere if he hadn't been so suspicious in the first place. It wasn't sexual liberation that ruined the relationship, it was distrust, brought on by insecurity, which created this self-fulfilling prophecy.

The question we must ask here is: do men have good reason to be suspicious in the first place? According to what I have learned from my interviews, the answer is a definitive "no." This point is well substantiated by other studies. In fact, of the approximately 3,000 single Americans polled in a recent nationwide study (the results of which were published in the book *Singles: The New Americans**) almost *90 percent of the women surveyed felt it was difficult or impossible to be "meaningfully and sexually involved with more than one person during the same period of time."*

It is time we put to rest the notion that the sexual revolution has turned the female populace into a bunch of free spirits, anxious to carry on a multitude of simultaneous love affairs. Men have no good reason not to trust their lovers, and suspicion can only bring about unnecessary damage to a relationship.

Some of you may notice that there is one disturbing question still to be answered: how does one account for those relationships in which the man *knows* from the start that his lover is sleeping with other men? In light of the above information, the woman's behavior should tell you something about how she views the relationship. Assuming she is not one of the 10 percent who feel they *can* be meaningfully and sexually involved with more than one man at the same time, we must conclude that although the relationship is clearly "sexual," in her mind it is not yet "meaningful"—or perhaps, more accurately, not meaningful *enough*. Still, there is no reason to be overly concerned with these circumstances at this point since, as I will discuss in detail later on, this behavior is more than likely to change once a woman has had more time to get to know you.

* Simenauer, J. and Carroll, D., *Singles: The New Americans*, New York: Simon and Schuster, 1982.

JUDGMENT DAY IS HERE

Because today's women are more sexually experienced and sexually aware than any of their predecessors, they may expect, or even demand more from their lovers—a fact which is giving today's men never-ending cause for concern. Yet although these women have a good basis for comparison, are they actually comparing the sexual prowess of their various lovers—cross-checking vital statistics and other pertinent information?

Not really. It is more accurate to say that women are *evaluating* the performance of their lovers, not comparing this performance to others. Unlike men, who tend to compare a woman's sexual skills to those of other women they have slept with, women approach sex with a far less comparison-oriented attitude. In other words, a woman will not ask herself, "Is this guy as good as Fred?", but instead, she is more apt to ask, "Does this man make me feel good in bed?" There is a significant difference in the implications of these two questions.

Still, we must recognize that there has to be some element of comparison in the woman's evaluation since her understanding of what makes her feel good in bed probably developed as a result of how Fred, Ted, or Ed made her feel in bed. But at the same time, it is equally plausible that her understanding developed as a result of how Fred, Ted, and Ed *didn't* make her feel in bed. For example, she may always have felt detached and/or depressed when she slept with them; now she wonders if she will feel the same way with you. If this is the case, she is not looking to see if you are as good a lover as the others were. Quite the contrary, she is hoping you will be very different, and that she will feel better with you. But what will make her feel better?

WHAT MAKES A MAN GOOD IN BED?

I have already pointed out that today's women are evaluating the performance of their lovers and expect a great deal from them. But what makes a man a good lover? Incredible staying power? Polished technique? Massive genitals? Although these are some of the answers men would expect women to give, women's actual responses again reflect something very different. Women tend to view sex as both a physical and emotional experience, and their complex needs reflect this. When asked, "What makes a man good in bed?", women consistently list characteristics such as: Attentiveness, consideration, caring, sensitivity, tenderness, warmth.

In addition, women also emphasize the importance of: Cuddling, hugging, caressing, touching, closeness, talking.

Various studies on women's sexual needs show the same results. In *The Hite Report*,* women rated emotional intimacy, tenderness, closeness, touching, and sensitivity as being far more pleasing than such things as intercourse

* Hite, S., *The Hite Report*, New York: Macmillan, 1976.

and cunnilingus (and you thought you knew everything about sex!).

Why the discrepancy between what men think women need in bed and what women really *do* need? Probably because of the nature of men's sexual needs. Since men place a tremendous amount of emphasis on a woman's sexual skills and physical characteristics, they naturally assume that women place an equal amount of emphasis on the same things. No way. According to women, *a good lover is an affectionate lover*, and even the most well-endowed, highly skilled bedroom athlete will find himself being rejected if he is not as affectionate as he is skilled.

Of course, a man's sexual skills *are* important to a woman—they are just far *less* important than everything else I've mentioned. In fact, if you had to break it down into percentages, I would estimate that as far as women are concerned, the mechanics of sex account for no more than 25 percent of a man's overall performance, while things like affection and tenderness acccount for at least 75 percent. I've even heard some women suggest that mechanics account for as little as 10 percent of a man's performance, but I think this may be downplaying their importance a little too much. After all, a basic understanding of the technical aspects of sex makes the experience somewhat more pleasurable, and certainly a lot less awkward—it is just that this knowledge alone is not sufficient.

What does all of this mean as far as you are concerned? If you want to be a good lover—since women *are* looking for good lovers—the first thing you must do is stop focusing on performance and start focusing on your feelings. Instead of tearing a woman's clothes off and diving under the covers with a miner's helmet on to look for her G-spot, start concentrating on showing your affection for her. If you don't have any, then you shouldn't be sleeping with her in the first place—you're definitely not doing her a favor, and you're probably not doing yourself one either.

4

Beyond the Pick-Up Scene

JUDGING from the questions I've been asked and the comments I've heard over the past few years, I often get the impression that half of men's troubles revolve around their inability to meet women (or perhaps more accurately, their inability to meet women successfully); nothing seems to cause more frustration. At the same time, however, women are constantly assuring me that they are very much interested in meeting men; in fact, they insist it is foolish for men to think otherwise. So why the contradiction? Probably because men are always trying to meet women in the wrong places, and with the wrong approach. Let's now take a closer look at each of these mistakes, and see what can be done to avoid them.

Searching for "Ms. Right"

THE WRONG PLACES

The search for a compatible female is never easy, but most men make it far more difficult than it has to be by always looking in the wrong places.

Singles' Bars

You've just finished a long, tough day at the office and you're feeling very sorry for yourself— work, work, work, and you haven't had a date in over a month. Even though you're exhausted, you force yourself to stop at a popular bar near your office; maybe tonight you'll get lucky. As usual, the bar is dark, crowded, and noisy. You squeeze your way through the crowd and finally get within shouting distance of the bartender. After finishing your first drink, you begin a casual 360-degree sweep of the room in search of prospects. Needless to say, you feel incredibly awkward the entire time, knowing that it is impossible for you not to look like someone who is "on the make."

A half hour passes with no results. Disgusted, you finish your second drink and start heading for the door. But on your way out, you spot someone out of the corner of your eye—an attractive brunette, sitting in a corner with another woman. You immediately panic, knowing there is only one thing worse than going to a bar and not seeing anyone you would like to meet: going to a bar and seeing someone you *would* like to meet.

Your first instinct is to keep walking out the door, but instead, you return to the bar for another drink. Now you have to make a decision: do you really want to meet her? One more careful look confirms your initial impression—she is definitely worth a try. So, the decision is made; but for some reason, your legs don't carry you across the room to her table. Instead, you remain at the bar, frozen in fear. This happens because a little game is now going on inside your head, a game that sounds something like this: "Should I approach her or shouldn't I? I'll hate myself if I don't . . . but what will I say? If she walks away, I'll feel like such a jerk, but if she doesn't. . . . Maybe I should send a drink to her table. No, she would probably think that was ridiculous. I'm just going to have to go over there. But what if she's a real bitch? Or worse, what if she's just not interested? If I don't try, I'll never know. But I feel so stupid walking over to her like this."

This goes on and on, driving you half insane. Sometimes, a final decision is reached within seconds, but typically, this mental struggle continues for fifteen or twenty minutes, if not more. By the time you've finally made up your mind, you're a complete wreck. Now, even if you do try to approach her, any attempt to make conversation is bound to be awkward, unnatural, and difficult to sustain—you're just too nervous.

Sound familiar? I'm not surprised. Despite a chronic lack of success, a substantial number of single men still find themselves drawn to typical pick-up places, such as bars and discos, whenever they feel the need to meet women. Considering the above scenario, one wonders why the bar scene continues to be so popular. Why would any man choose to spend his time in an environment where pressure, superficiality, competition, and rejection fears make socializing a nightmare?

Judging from the opinions of the many men I have spoken with, there seem to be two answers to this question. On the one hand, there are those who are undaunted by the above-mentioned obstacles. These men firmly believe that if they are willing to guts it out, it is only a question of time before their luck changes. On the other hand, there are those who are not so optimistic, but who continue to frequent bars anyway for lack of a better alternative.

But all of these men are probably wasting their time, for the bar scene offers little hope for the man who is searching for "Ms. Right." This is because men are not the only ones plagued by problems in this environment; women also have their share of troubles to contend with—some far more serious. As a result, they are becoming less and less receptive to meeting men under such circumstances. In fact, many women have abandoned the bar scene entirely—especially those women who are looking for a more meaningful relationship than the bar scene tends to offer (the same women you are hoping to find).

To better understand why the pick-up environment is turning women off, it is helpful to become more familiar with the problems that are affecting their behavior, especially since these problems have also become our problems.

Bad Connotations. For some women, the bad connotations surrounding singles' bars are enough to keep them away. But what about the women who still go to bars—are they completely unaffected by these negative connotations? Hardly. No woman wants to think of herself as being an easy pick-up, and as a result, even the women who frequent such places often resist men's advances. In essence, they are making a statement: "Listen buddy, just because I'm here, it doesn't mean I'm an easy pick-up." Although this attitude may make a woman feel better about being in this type of environment, it can drive men up the wall. To illustrate, I would like to share with you an experience I had several years ago in a popular New York disco (yes, I used to go to discos just like everyone else):

Driven by boredom, a few friends and I decided one evening to take a look at a new discotheque which had opened on Manhattan's upper east side. As soon as we entered, we knew we had made a mistake; unfortunately, we had already paid the astronomical cover charge. The place was crammed full of bodies (most of them were still breathing), and the music was pouring out of the loudspeakers at an intolerably high level, rendering any attempt to make conversation futile. Looking around for potential dance partners, I soon spotted a woman who was standing on the edge of the dance floor swaying to the music. This girl definitely wanted to dance. But as I was desperately elbowing my way through the crowd to get to her, another man who had been standing closer to her asked her to dance. Luckily (or so I thought), she must have refused, because he quickly turned and walked away. After a little more squeezing, pushing, and shoving, I finally reached her; but when I asked her to dance, she refused, explaining that she was going to be leaving shortly. But she didn't leave shortly; she stayed, fixed in that same spot, swaying to the music for at least another hour. During that hour, she must have turned down almost ten other men who asked her to dance. I watched this with great curiosity, dying to ask her, "Why are you here?" Finally she left, never having danced with anyone.

Perhaps this woman's behavior was a bit extreme, even for the bar scene, but here is a much more typical example of the way women resist being picked up in pick-up places:

You're having a drink at your favorite bar, eyeing the door, hoping that someone interesting will walk in. Suddenly, not one, but two attractive women come through the door together. You immediately decide it must be your lucky night. When the women walk past you, you smile, but they seem not to notice; still, you're not discouraged. They sit down at a nearby table, and immediately become engrossed in conversation. Your mind starts buzzing. What should you do? Send drinks to their table? No—too corny. Send a note to their table? No—too weird. Best to just walk over to them and say hello before someone else does. Mustering up all of the courage you've got, you stand up, stride over to their table, introduce yourself, and ask if you can buy them a drink. They thank you, but decline your offer. Put off, but not defeated, you then ask if you could pull up a chair and join them. They turn down your request, offering some feeble excuse. Suddenly you feel very foolish. Unable to think of anything else to say, you turn and head back to your seat. For two hours, they remain in the bar, talking only with each other. Any man who tries to break into their conversation receives the same treatment you received. As you watch these women, you can't help wondering why they are there. If they just wanted to talk, why did they choose a crowded singles' bar, with so many quieter places available? They had to know that they were going to be constantly interrupted by the many men surrounding them.

Why did they go to a singles' bar? Because they wanted to meet men. Once inside, however, they were trapped by their own conflicting impulses, and ended up fighting the stigmas of the pick-up environment by refusing to be picked up. At the end of this unsuccessful evening, they leave with an even greater distaste for the bar scene. This means that the next time they go (and they *will* go again if they can't find an alternative), they will be even less receptive to meeting anyone.

Pressure. Not only does the meat-market atmosphere of singles' bars and discos make women extremely uncomfortable, but it also pressures them to pass immediate judgment on every man who crosses their path. Before a man can even open his mouth to say "hello," a woman's decision-making process has begun. First, she will quickly evaluate you to decide whether or not she is willing to talk to you at all. Since this decision is usually made in a dark, crowded, noisy, tense environment, you can be sure that it will be based on all of the wrong things—namely, your superficial characteristics (what other choice does she have?). You can also be sure that she is apt to be far more critical in this environment than she would be anywhere else.

Sometimes you will get lucky enough to get a few minutes of conversation in, but then another series of evaluations is made. This time, she may be asking herself: "Do I want to talk to this guy all night? Do I want to talk to him at all? Are there more interesting prospects around? Is he going to ask for my phone number? Do I feel like giving it to him? Is he going to ask me for a date? Do I want to bother? Is he going to try to take me home tonight? Do I want to go?" The pressure to answer these questions, and answer them quickly (long before she knows very much about you), invariably leads to rejection.

Personal Safety. One of the most important, and most overlooked drawbacks to the pick-up environment is the problem of personal safety—and I don't mean yours. The vast majority of men (who never entertain thoughts of rape or bondage) may find this hard to believe, but virtually all of the women I have ever interviewed have admitted that concern for their personal safety strongly affects their attitude toward meeting strangers in a singles' bar. These women have told me that the thought of going home with, going out with, or even giving their phone number to a man they've met in a bar can conjure up all kinds of frightening images in their minds—images which are constantly reinforced by the media's never-ending coverage of rapes, beatings, slayings, venereal diseases, and a variety of other social ills.

Are these images realistic, or just a product of media distortions? Many men would like to believe the latter, but the statistics tell us otherwise. After all, how can we blame the media for putting unrealistic notions into women's heads when studies of single women reveal that *more than one third* of the women who go to singles' bars have been victims of some form of physical or mental abuse which resulted from their visits to these bars.

No wonder women are not so receptive to meeting men in bars;they have a lot to worry about. These worries make women excessively critical and cautious, as evidenced by the following typical behavior patterns:

The women you meet in bars refuse to go home with you

or

they refuse to accept a date with you

or

they accept dates, but they don't show up or they cancel at the last minute

or

they refuse to give you their phone numbers, or give you phony ones.

Most of us are familiar with some or all of these patterns. Some of us have blamed ourselves for eliciting these reactions; others have blamed women. What I hope you now see is that the blame is neither ours nor theirs—it is the environment which is causing most of the problems.

There is one more drawback to singles' bars: the problem of the one-night stand. If, by some stroke of luck, you successfully pick up a woman at a singles' bar, perhaps the worst thing you can do is try to convince her to go home with you. On the one hand, there is a very good chance that your overtures will offend or insult the woman ("He thinks I'm easy"); if this is the case, don't expect to see her again. On the other hand, if she accepts your invitation (yes, this is possible—although the popularity of the one-night stand has decreased dramatically, there are still a few women who don't object to finding a warm body to keep them company for the night), your worst troubles may just be starting. As you might suspect, I am referring to the problem of sexual pressure. This will be discussed in detail later on, but for now it is important to bear in mind that sleeping with a woman you have just picked-up in a bar maximizes your chance of encountering uncomfortable, if not devastating, sexual pressure (not to mention the risk you take of picking up something else, such as one of those nasty diseases we keep reading about).

The Street

It's a beautiful, sunny autumn afternoon, and you decide it would be a shame to waste it sitting at home watching sitcom reruns. Why not go into town and do some pre-Christmas window shopping?

Once in town, you can't help noticing how many attractive women are out shopping. You feel like a little kid in a candy store. Trying to concentrate on your shopping, you walk from store to store until you spot something in a window that you think you'd like to buy. But as you're about to walk into the store, you glimpse the sleek figure of a tall brunette rushing past you. You turn just in time to get a good look at her, and what you see looks a lot more interesting than what you were looking at in the store window.

With no time to lose, you take off down the street after her, but as you're gaining on her, it dawns on you that you have no idea what to say when you reach her. Finally a light bulb goes on in your head; you open the band of your wristwatch, and slip the watch off your wrist and into your pocket. Moments later, you're close enough to stop her, so you call out, "Excuse me . . . do you know what time it is?"

She stops and turns toward you, but she does not greet you with the friendly smile you had anticipated (already you can tell that she is annoyed that you stopped her, and that she probably realizes you don't really care what time it is). She takes a quick look at her watch, tells you the time, turns, and walks away twice as fast as she was walking before. As you watch her race away from you, something tells you not to waste any more time pursuing her.

This familiar scenario is here to remind you that if there is one thing harder than trying to meet women in singles' bars, it is trying to pick them up on the street. There are several reasons why this approach constantly fails:

- There is nothing natural or comfortable about stopping a woman on the street and trying to start a conversation. It usually necessitates the use of some contrived pick-up line which is certain to turn most women off immediately (I will discuss the drawbacks of the pick-up line shortly).
- Even if, by some unlikely stroke of luck, you are able to stop a woman on the street, she is not likely to remain stopped for very long—certainly not long enough for you to have a productive conversation: it is far too easy and too desirable for her to walk away.
- Women—especially those in big cities—don't like being stopped on the street by strange men. This aversion to being stopped begins in childhood, brought on by the familiar parental warning, "Don't talk to strangers!" As a woman gets older, these warnings may move into the recesses of her subconscious mind, but her aversion to strange men does not. Instead, it is continually reinforced as she learns to ignore the comments, jeers, and leers of the many men she passes on the street on a given day. Ultimately, being stopped on the street becomes the very essence of what women have learned to fear and avoid.
- The only time a woman *may* stop to talk for any length of time is when she is immediately, and strongly

attracted to the man who stops her. But what will this attraction be based on? Your charming personality? No chance. Under these circumstances, a man's superficial qualities determine his fate—there just isn't enough time for other, more important qualities to show through. This puts the vast majority of us at a disadvantage, especially since women are prone to being far more critical under these circumstances than they would be normally. As one friend of mine remarked, "If Paul Newman stops me on the street, I'll talk to him. Otherwise, forget it!"

The combination of these four drawbacks makes it difficult for even the most confident, aggressive men to meet women on the street, a point inadvertently, but clearly illustrated by the story a young New York businessman shared with one of my "FOR MEN ONLY" classes. It seems that every morning before work, this man hangs around the subway station exit near his office, waiting to pounce (although I use the word figuratively, after hearing the description of his approach, I couldn't think of a better verb) on any attractive prospects who happen to be exiting the station that morning. He boasted to the class that he has had tremendous success with this pick-up approach.

Knowing how the average New York female would react to someone so indiscreet, I suspected that this man was stretching the truth. Instead of challenging him, however, I urged him to give us more details of his successes. He then proudly told the class that out of every *ten* women he approached, *one* would usually stop to talk with him.

He then added that almost 50 percent of the women who stopped would agree to meet him later for a drink. Of those who accepted his invitation, approximately 75 percent showed up. Some success story! A few quick calculations told me that *only one out of every twenty-five* women he approached on the street wound up meeting him later on. That's a lot of rejections to handle for just one drink. Imagine how many times you would be turned down before you met someone who was willing to go out with you more than once. No wonder he had signed up for my class.

This businessman's "success" story is all the more proof that there is nothing more difficult than trying to pick up women on the street. But if the women who pass you by on the street are off-limits, and if the bar scene is a disaster, where *can* you meet women successfully?

THE RIGHT PLACES

Once you have decided to leave the pick-up scene behind, you will discover that there are an unlimited number of places where you can meet your type of women—many places which you've probably overlooked for years. In the next few pages, I have listed many of these, grouping them according to the relative ease of meeting women in each place (based on the number of women available, the receptivity of the women in that particular environment, the ease of starting a conversation under those circumstances, etc.). As you read through these examples, the most important things to keep in mind are:

- You want to meet women in an environment that shows you off at your best.
- You want to meet women in an environment that maximizes your opportunity to talk—the more a woman can get to know you, the more likely she is to want to see you again.
- The less any place resembles a pick-up environment, the greater your chances of successfully meeting women there.

Very Good

Some of the best places to meet women include the workplace, school (college, graduate school, adult education classes, etc.), and special interest groups. Though these three types of environments are quite different, they all share two characteristics which make them ideal for meeting women:

1. *Common Interests*

Unlike the women you try to stop on the street or pick up in a bar, the women you meet at work, at school, or through special interest groups already share some of your interests. Not only does this give you something to talk about, but this bond also makes a woman perceive you as less of a stranger. A woman is likely to be far more willing to get to know you under such circumstances.

2. *Repeated Contact*

Another advantage of these places is that your opportunities will usually knock more than once—if you see a woman one time, chances are, you will see her many times. This puts less pressure on you to force a conversation or a pick-up the first time you notice someone; if a good opportunity to meet doesn't present itself, you can simply wait until one does. This is quite unlike the "now or never" pressure of the bar scene.

In addition, repeated contact gives you the opportunity to become more well-acquainted with a woman without having to begin the dating ritual. As you will see later, this is a big plus.

With these two advantages in mind, let's now examine each of the above-mentioned meeting environments.

The workplace. Today, more than ever before, the workplace provides single men with some of their best opportunities to meet women. Certainly there are occupational hazards (and I don't mean asbestos poisoning), but there will be many women crossing your path in the workplace who don't present much of a job risk, including women who work in adjacent offices or on other floors in your building (you know, the ones you always see in the elevator), as well as those whose work brings them through your office periodically, such as the sales reps, purchasing agents, advertising executives, lawyers, and artists. As long as you don't have a close working relationship with any of them, feel free to choose. (For more on this, see "Office Romance: What are the risks?" in Chapter 9.)

School. To many of us, it seems as though our social lives took a nose dive the day we left school. It was so easy then; so many women, that we took most of them for granted . . . so many dates, that the weekend never seemed long enough to accommodate all our plans. Although many of us long for those "good old days," very few of us try to re-create that environment. I'm not suggesting that you re-enroll in college, but I am recommending that you do the next best thing: take advantage of your local adult education program.

Almost every town in the United States has one or more adult ed programs which offer courses in the evenings and on weekends, and if you select the right courses, adult education can open up a whole new social life for you. But what distinguishes the right courses from the wrong courses? The right courses . . .

> *. . . have as many, or more, women than men.*
>
> Try to find courses which tend to have at least as many women enrolled as men (if not more). Looking through a course catalog, it should be fairly easy to spot courses which fit this description. Some of the better choices are usually cooking classes, exercise classes, dance classes, and art classes (of course you can never be 100 percent certain, but you can make an educated guess).
>
> If meeting women is priority number one, then you might want to avoid classes such as auto mechanics, body-building, and investment strategies. There may be women in these classes, but they will probably be far outnumbered by the men.

Of course, if you have absolutely no interest in the subject matter of a course, it is not advisable to sign up for it *only* because you think there will be women in the class. There is never any guarantee that you will meet someone, and you will feel you have wasted a lot of time and money if you don't. Pick courses you think you would enjoy regardless of whether or not Ms. Right shows up; this way, you can never be totally disappointed.

. . . have hands-on experience.

If you sign up for a lecture course, you may find yourself trapped in a seat in the corner of an auditorium, listening to a boring lecturer for three hours. Even if there are any women sitting near you, it may be awkward or impossible to carry on a conversation with them. After all, they are there to hear the lecturer, not to hear you (a point they may remind you of if you attempt to talk to them). On the other hand, a course that offers hands-on experience in the classroom is ideal for meeting women. With all of the activity, and with the need to usually work with partners or in groups, it is often necessary, and always easy, to converse with the women in the class.

Therefore, for example, don't sign up for a lecture course on "The History of Italian Cuisine"; sign up instead for a hands-on course like "Pasta Making." As you run around the classroom breaking eggs, kneading dough, and playing with all the funny machines, you'll have dozens of chances to meet and talk to any number of women.

Other good hands-on courses include acting classes and recreational athletics (tennis for beginners, skating for beginners, etc.)—just check a course catalog to see what is offered where you live.

. . . meet more than once.

If a course only meets once, you may feel the same way you did back in that pick-up bar—pressured to make a move because you think you'll never see the woman again otherwise. But if a course meets more than once, you are under no pressure to immediately force a conversation. Instead, you can let your face become a familiar one, and eventually start a conversation when you have a reasonable opportunity to do so—even if you have to wait until the second or third class (or even the fourth or fifth).

One more thing . . . before you immerse yourself in the world of adult education, you should be aware of two rules of thumb:

1. Never act like you're on the make.

If you cruise around the classroom as though you were in a singles' bar, you will turn a lot of women off. The last thing you want to do is create a pick-up atmosphere in what should be a relaxed, pressure-free environment.

2. Always be friendly.

Even if Ms. Right didn't sign up for the course you chose, always be friendly to the other people in the class. You never know who may have a nice friend.

Special interest groups. Another very successful method of meeting women is through special interest groups. In such groups, you will constantly be meeting women who have a great deal in common with you; as I said before, this is likely to make them far more interested in getting to know you.

I cannot begin to count the number of couples I know who have met in this fashion. One couple, who met during a political campaign in Boston, told me they know of at least three other relationships that developed out of that same campaign. They tell all their single friends, "If you want to meet someone, get involved in politics—even if you're not interested in politics." Of course, there are other things to get involved in aside from political campaigns, including: religious organizations, singles' workshops, conservation groups, cooking clubs, and athletic groups, just to name a few.

What about health clubs? Recently, health clubs have been getting a lot of press. Most of it, of course, revolves around the boom in health-mindedness, but some of it examines the health club from another angle—as the "singles' bar of the 80s." It is true that many people are turning to their local health club for social, as well as health-related reasons, but are these clubs the ideal place to meet women? As you might suspect, the social benefits of the health club seem to be diminishing in direct proportion to the increase in publicity touting this style of social interaction. This is because the label, "singles' bar of the 80s," is becoming a self-fulfilling prophecy—men are beginning to act as though they *were* in a bar ("Hey, can I buy you a glass of carrot juice?"), and women, once unsuspecting of the friendly guy who helped them use the nautilus equipment, now fear that every man who comes within twenty feet of them is trying to pick them up.

Of course, health clubs are not as bad as singles' bars (not yet, anyway), but if you hope to successfully mix athletics with socializing, it is recommended that you avoid any club which has developed a reputation as being a "hard-core" singles' hang-out. Instead, look for a club where you can still be "the nice guy who just wants to help the woman next to him use the nautilus equipment."

Good

Any place with a captive audience. Have you ever noticed how easy it is to strike up a conversation with a woman sitting next to you on an airplane? Why is this so? Does the excitement of flying make women more sociable? Do high altitudes reduce their inhibitions? Perhaps one day a study will explore these possibilities, but I tend to think there is a far more simple explanation. It all relates to the phenomenon of the captive audience. You see, once you are strapped in for a two-hour flight, the woman next to you is bound to quickly realize that you are her travel companion, whether she likes it or not. Forced to choose between reading the in-flight magazine five times, and talking to you, most women will opt for the latter.

Does this mean that if you want to meet women you have to call your travel agent? Certainly not (unless, of course, you happen to be attracted to your travel agent); the principles of the captive audience work as well on the ground as they do in the air. *Any* situation which provides you with a captive audience also provides you with a good opportunity to meet someone new because:

- You have plenty of time to talk—time for the woman you are "holding hostage" to get to know you better.
- You are not pressured to make a quick pick-up; instead, you can relax and have a pleasant conversation, devoid of any pick-up overtones.
- It is awkward, and often impossible for a woman to walk away, and it is uncomfortable for her to ignore you (unlike singles' bars, where it is socially acceptable to ignore *everyone* who tries to talk to you).

Where are you most likely to find yourself in the company of a captive audience? Here are a few possibilities:

- Waiting rooms—doctors' offices, business offices, hospital waiting rooms (if you're really desperate), etc.
- Long lines—cafeteria lines, theater lines, lines inside crowded restaurants, etc. (if you're not standing next to anyone interesting, give up your place and try again).
- Restaurant counters—luncheonettes, sushi bars, etc. (make sure you don't sit next to someone who is about to leave).
- Various forms of transportation—boats, planes, trains, etc. (excluding some forms of public transportation, such as subways); the longer the trip, the better.

Social functions. Social functions provide many men with some of their best opportunities to meet women. At the same time, however, some men never seem to be able to meet women at such functions. Why the discrepancy? Well, these functions *can* be very good places to meet women, but only if one of the following criteria are met:

• *There aren't too many guests.*

The smaller the function, the better it is for you. Although it may be difficult to meet anyone at a lawn party where there are 200 guests, it is fairly easy to meet someone at a dinner party for fifteen people.

• *You know the host(ess), and the host(ess) knows all the guests.*

Even if a party is fairly large, you still have an opportunity to meet a lot of women, provided that you know the host, and the host knows all of the guests. This way, even if you don't have the opportunity to meet anyone *during* the party, you can always ask the host at some later time to introduce you to whomever caught your eye at the party.

Fair

Supermarkets and department stores. Recently a lot of attention has been given to books and courses which teach men how to meet women in places such as supermarkets and department stores. Although such environments are far superior to the bar scene, they do have their drawbacks:

• It is sometimes difficult to approach a woman in this type of environment without appearing as though you are trying to make a pick-up.

• These situations do not usually provide you with a captive audience; if a woman isn't immediately interested, there is nothing to stop her from walking away.

• Since you have no assurance of ever seeing the woman again, there is a lot of pressure on you to force a meeting, even if the circumstances are far less than ideal.

Museums. Museums used to be fairly good places to meet women, but all of the press surrounding this once-popular meeting place has put many women on their guard. The result? That depends on the woman, but don't be surprised if you don't get the warm reception you would have received five or ten years ago (in addition, museums are also a little too quiet to make them ideal places for having a conversation—especially if a woman is not that anxious to talk in the first place).

The preceding list is by no means 100 percent inclusive. Its purpose is to show that there are an unlimited number of different types of meeting environments, all of which are far superior to a typical pick-up environment. But this information alone is not enough; now that you know *where* to meet women, you have to know *how*. . . .

How to Approach Women

THE WRONG WAY

Although a lot of men claim they have abandoned the bar scene (I use the word "claim," since I have yet to hear any singles' bar owners complain of dramatic losses in revenue), many seem not to realize that *how* they try to meet women is as important as *where* they try to meet women. Let me illustrate:

You're at the local supermarket, stocking up on groceries for the weekend. As you are waiting to be served at the deli counter, an attractive woman wheels her shopping cart past you. Watching her go by, you can't help being reminded that you have no plans for the weekend. A few minutes later, as you are wheeling your cart past the canned goods, you see her again. This time, she is standing in front of the seven-foot-tall display of coffee cans, trying to figure out how to get one of the cans off the top of the pile. After a few moments of deliberation, you decide that she would probably appreciate a chivalrous gesture. But before you have a chance to offer any assistance, she decides to take a gamble and remove one of the cans from the bottom of the pile. Suddenly, hundreds of coffee cans come crashing to the ground; her face turns beet-red with embarrassment. Figuring that you now have an even better excuse to approach her, you walk over and begin picking up some of the cans. She smiles, thanks you, and continues picking up the cans. Not wanting to miss out on this opportunity to start a conversation, you turn to her and say, "Don't I know you from somewhere?"

A slight exaggeration? Perhaps—but I think you see the point: men tend to rely so heavily on memorized pick-up lines that they are often oblivious to more natural, more successful ways of starting a conversation.

If pick-up lines were as foolproof as some people claim, I would have no reason to criticize their use. But the truth is that a lot of women are instantly turned off by this approach. In fact, the only place where pick-up lines still retain any margin of acceptability is in pick-up places—the same places I've just given you a dozen reasons to avoid.

Why do women react so negatively to pick-up lines? First of all, every woman has heard all of the standard lines a thousand times, and unless a woman is extremely naive (though I fail to believe any woman can be *that* naive), she will immediately label you as insincere (or worse). This is a bad way to try to start a relationship—displaying one of your worst qualities before you've had a chance to show any of your best.

In addition, the use of a pick-up line immediately changes the tone of your encounter; what could have been a low-pressure first meeting, quickly becomes a high-pressure pick-up. There is a big difference between the two; once a woman senses that you are trying to pick her up, she is apt to immediately put her guard up and become more skeptical, more critical, and far less receptive to meeting you.

But if using a pick-up line is the wrong way to approach a woman, what is the right way?

THE RIGHT WAY

The right way to approach a woman depends a lot on whether you will have one, or more than one opportunity to meet her. Let me explain:

If you think you will have several opportunities to meet a woman (she works in your office, she lives in your apartment building, she's enrolled in a course with you), sometimes the best thing to do the first time you see her is to simply smile and say "hello"—especially if the situation makes it awkward for you to start a conversation (she's running out the door to catch a bus; she's with another guy). Many men are under the mistaken impression that they *must* try to start a conversation with a woman the first time they see her, regardless of whether or not they'll be seeing her again. This attitude can hurt a lot more than it can help.

All you really need to do the first time you see a woman is try to break the ice a little. By smiling and saying hello, you are establishing yourself as a friendly face (not as a man on the prowl); the next time you see her, it will be that much easier for you to start a conversation. Of course, if a decent chance to speak does not present itself the second time you see her, there is no reason to panic. Just continue to be friendly, and wait for an appropriate opportunity to come along. When it does, you'll be glad you waited.

But what if you think you have only one chance to meet the woman (those "do or die" situations that never fail to put a knot in our stomachs)? Smiling and saying hello may be very nice gestures, but they're not going to trigger a lengthy conversation (not usually, anyway). Besides, even if you see a woman all of the time, you can't smile and say hello forever—sooner or later you're going to have to start a conversation. So what do you do? Is there *one* correct thing to say? Absolutely not. Since every woman and every set of circumstances is unique, the proper approach is always going to be different. So instead of giving you a list of snappy phrases or clever gimmicks to rely on, here is a series of suggestions which will help you develop your own style—one that is flexible enough to accommodate a variety of different circumstances, and at the same time, suited to your unique personality:

Be Friendly

Commenting on how difficult it was to meet women, a friend once remarked, "I guess I have to learn to be more aggressive." "No you don't," I replied, "you just have to learn to be friendly."

If you want to meet women, *a friendly smile and an easygoing attitude are your most valuable assets.* Although many women are turned off by slick, aggressive men, almost no woman is turned off by a man who is genuinely friendly.

Pay Attention to the Circumstances

Stop fishing for clever pick-up lines, and start paying attention to the surrounding circumstances. Many men are so programmed to use the standard lines that they never notice (or never look for) the things a woman would be interested in talking about (remember the supermarket story). Just keep your eyes and ears open and you will be provided with plenty of natural opportunities to start a conversation, be it about the weather, the economy, or the stain on your tie.

Pay Attention to the Woman

If you are observant, you will notice many things about a woman which can help you start a conversation:

- If the woman is wearing an unusual piece of clothing or jewelry that attracts your attention, ask her about it: "That's a beautiful pendant; I've never seen anything quite like it. Did you buy it around here?" or "That's a great-looking scarf—would you mind telling me who the designer is? Does he (she) make scarves for men?" Questions such as these are flattering to the woman, and also encourage conversation.
- Perhaps the woman is carrying something of interest to you, such as a new type of camera. Ask her about it: Is she happy with it? . . . Does she find it very easy to use, or is it too complicated? . . . Would she recommend it to someone else? She will probably be happy to tell you all about it, and your conversation can continue from there.

Say What's on Your Mind

It is often easiest, and most effective to simply say what is on your mind (within reason, of course):

• You arrive at your attorney's office for a meeting, only to be greeted by half a dozen other people in the waiting room, including one woman who immediately catches your eye. Instead of wondering to yourself how long you'll have to wait, *ask her*: has she been waiting long? . . . Does she have any idea how much longer you may have to wait? Once she answers you, just continue the conversation.

• You're on a train, going to visit some friends. At one stop, a pleasant looking woman gets on and sits down a few seats away from you. Perhaps you are wondering what time the train will arrive at your stop. Instead of fiddling with the train schedule for half an hour, *ask her*. Even if she doesn't know, you have still broken the ice, and continuing a conversation should be easy (especially since you have a captive audience).

• You've signed up for an Oriental cooking course and you are struggling to put your newly acquired information to work (to wok?). Perhaps you could ask the woman next to you why her egg foo young looks so much more appetizing than yours. . . . Has she ever studied Chinese cooking before?. . . Where? . . . Does she know of a good place to buy the special ingredients?

Ask a Question

You will notice that in the preceding examples, the conversation openers all take the form of questions. Making a statement can lead to a nod of agreement, but it doesn't always encourage a woman to talk. Asking a question encourages conversation—especially if the question can't be answered with one or two words. Of course, if you can't immediately think of a question, it is better to make a statement than to say nothing—remember, your goal is to make conversation.

Don't Hesitate

Once you have an opportunity to start a conversation, don't procrastinate. The longer you wait, the harder it gets; wait too long, and the psychological barriers become overwhelming (both for you, *and* for her).

Many men are guilty of waiting too long. Instead of saying the first thig that comes to their minds, they waste precious time racking their brains in search of something brilliant to say. But every second that passes makes the situation more strained, and most men discover that it only takes a few minutes before the situation has gone into deep freeze. At that point, even the best lines probably won't be able to break the ice.

If you want to start a successful conversation, stop worrying so much about what you're going to say, and just start talking. Even if your first few sentences aren't one tenth as witty or intelligent as you would like them to be, it doesn't really matter—after five minutes of friendly chatter, the woman probably won't even remember how the conversation got started (unless, of course, you used a stock pick-up line—but in that case, the conversation probably won't last five minutes anyway).

Use Humor

Humor always helps; don't be afraid to use it. But remember two things:

- Don't sit in silence for twenty minutes trying to think of a humorous opening line. If something funny doesn't pop into your head right away, just start a straight, friendly conversation.
- Women may laugh at your jokes, but jokes don't always encourage conversation. A friend of mine used to have a tremendous knack for making women laugh; but instead of trying to talk to the women a while, he would just keep making jokes. Eventually, the women would tire and walk away. It took him a long time to realize that the goal is to talk to women, not to entertain them. Learn from his mistakes—after you've broken the ice with a joke or two, make sure to follow up with some friendly dialogue.

Be Spontaneous

The preceding examples of conversation openers are just *examples*—do not try to memorize them. Memorized lines always *sound* like memorized lines and that can be a big turn off. Women respond to spontaneity.

Be Yourself

I have saved this for last because it is, by far, the most important point. You are not Humphrey Bogart— DON'T TRY TO ACT LIKE HIM! Women are most attracted to a man who has the confidence to just be himself. The more natural you are, the easier it will be for you to meet women—regardless of the circumstances.

THROUGH INTRODUCTION

Believe it or not, over half of the women I have spoken with told me they still meet most of the men they date through some sort of introduction. If no one has ever offered to introduce you to anyone, it is probably because you haven't asked—no one is going to place a list of names and phone numbers in your lap if you don't make it very clear that you are looking. Furthermore, telling only one or two of your best friends is not enough; you have to tap *all* of your resources. Tell everyone—your family, friends, business contacts, acquaintances—then let these people tell other people; you will be amazed by the results networking can bring. One friend of mine, finding himself suddenly single, told almost everyone he knew that he was interested in meeting someone. Within two weeks, he had received half a dozen names and numbers—friends of friends, friends of friends of friends, cousins of friends, etc. After three weeks, his list had doubled. Six months later, he moved in with one of the women from the list.

In addition to being easy, this approach has several other advantages:

- Meeting this way doesn't have any bad connotations.
- Meeting this way minimizes a woman's concern for

her personal safety (she assumes her friends wouldn't set her up with a creep).

• You immediately have something in common with the woman you are introduced to, namely, the person who did the introducing.

One more word of advice. If someone wants to introduce you to a woman, ask them to set it up as a low-pressure introduction, not a blind date. Many women are automatically turned off by the words "blind date," and will refuse to meet you under such circumstances.

THROUGH THE CLASSIFIEDS

When I first set out to write this book I did not intend to discuss the merits and drawbacks of meeting women through the classified ads in newspapers and magazines—especially since only a small fraction of men and women take advantage of this method of introduction. But as I started teaching my "FOR MEN ONLY" seminars, I quickly realized that peoples' interest in the use of personal ads was growing. In fact, almost every time I lecture on the wheres and hows of meeting women, someone asks me my opinion of meeting through the classifieds.

Are personal ads the long-awaited solution to all the problems most men experience trying to meet Ms. Right? Well, the use of these ads certainly has its advantages—it can save a lot of time and money, it lets you look or ask for exactly what you want (although there is no guarantee you'll get it), it is a lot less awkward than several other popular methods of meeting women, and it doesn't demand a tremendous effort on your part. As one man insisted, "It's easier than everything else!"

It is still too early to pass any kind of judgment on the value of the classifieds (especially since the stigma surrounding their use is only now beginning to disappear), but here is some information which will make it easier for you to decide whether or not you might benefit from placing or answering a personal ad:

Placing an Ad

I recently sat in on a course offered in New York City which teaches single men and women better ways to meet other singles. Midway through the seminar, the instructor brought up the topic of personal ads. After briefly discussing the use of these ads, she asked if anyone was willing to tell the class about any experiences they had placing or answering ads. I didn't expect anyone to respond to the question, so you can imagine how surprised I was when several hands went up. First, a young woman told how she had placed an ad in a New York newspaper and received almost 200 responses. She admitted that many of them were odd—a few even frightening—but many fell within her definition of normal. I found the details of her story fascinating, though I couldn't help but be somewhat bothered; here she was with 200 responses sitting on her desk at home, but she was still attending a course on how to meet people in New York. Obviously, she had failed to find Mr. Right among her responses. When this woman finished her story, a second woman spoke. Her ad drew almost 400 responses!

A man in the class had also placed an ad recently in the same paper the two women used. His return, however, was not a staggering 400, nor even a hefty 200. He received *seventeen* responses. At first, I wondered whether or not the wording of his ad was responsible for not stimulating much interest. Did he for example, say he was:

> Looking for dominant female—6′6″ or taller—blonde hair, blue eyes only—must wear size nine shoes or larger?

I suspected not. What I did suspect was that women are more inclined to *place* ads than to answer them. I have since discovered that my hunch was correct. In *Classified Love: A Guide to the Personals,** author Sherri Foxman points out that men's responses to women's ads generally outnumber women's responses to men's ads *thirty to one.* Therefore, if you're considering placing an ad, don't expect to be buried under your mail for the next six months.

Answering an Ad

I was recently a guest on a nationwide radio program which confronts the problems between the sexes. During

* Foxman, S., *Classified Love: A Guide to the Personals,* New York: McGraw-Hill, 1982.

the show, I was asked to give my opinion of personal ads. After the taping, I was stopped by a man outside the studio who had been listening; he told me that one year ago he had become brave enough to answer a few ads. His first two attempts were disappointing, but the third was not—he met a woman whom he has been seeing ever since. I asked him if he had ever placed an ad, and he told me he didn't think it was necessary since there were so many ads to answer. He discovered what I had surmised: men tend to benefit more from answering ads than from placing them.

One thing to remember: if you ever decide to place or answer an ad, don't expect miracles. Like every other approach to meeting women, the use of the classifieds has its drawbacks. Even the author of *Classified Love* would have to admit this, especially since she informs us in her introduction that, "During the past two years I placed a dozen ads for myself and received several thousand responses. I dated some of the respondents, but so far I haven't found Mr. Right. I'm still looking, and still placing ads."

Now that you have a better grasp of the wheres and hows of meeting women, the next logical question you should ask is, "What do you do once you've met someone?" But everybody knows the answer to that . . . you call her and ask her out on a date, right? WRONG. . . .

5

To Date, or Not to Date?

Now that self-sufficiency has freed women from the traditional constraints of male dependency, women can take their time, be selective, and resist settling for anything less than what they want. In terms of dating, this means that the new woman is not interested and not pressured to date any half-decent prospect who comes along. Instead, she may only be willing to date the handful of men who immediately meet her standards. But even these men cannot let themselves be lulled into a false sense of security, for the screening process has just begun. These days, few women view dating as a pleasant way of getting to know someone. Instead, dating has become a vehicle for conducting a series of highly critical evaluations of compatibility, where one disappointing evening in the beginning stages of a relationship can be grounds for termination.

This hardly seems fair, especially since we are all aware

of how people's feelings and perceptions can change dramatically once they have the chance to get to know someone better. But today, women seem unwilling to give men that chance. Why have women become so difficult? Because the dating process is no longer a source of pleasure for these women, but instead, a never-ending source of pressures and problems.

The Dating Timetable

Many of women's confusing, seemingly unpredictable reactions to the dating game become easier to understand, and perhaps, not so unpredictable, when viewed as different reactions to the same problem: sex. Dating has become an unending source of sexual pressure, and at the heart of this problem lies the "dating timetable"—the concept that sex is expected to become an integral part of the dating process after only one or two dates.

Why is this timetable a problem? Because a woman's decision to sleep with a man is a very personal, emotionally complex decision that has little or nothing to do with the number of times she has dated him. Granted, some women may be ready to sleep with a man after knowing him for only a few days, but others may not be ready for weeks or months. Yet the dating timetable does not account for this. Ready or not, the pressure starts, and a woman quickly finds herself forced to make an unpleasant decision: Does she reject a man's advances and spend an unpleasant evening arguing about it, or does she give in and spend another depressing night in the arms of a stranger? The choices are not pleasant.

In light of this, it should come as no surprise that many women, sick of the pressures of this timetable, are creating a third option for themselves: they are opting out. Women are turning off—if they are not ready to sleep with a man after one or two dates, the next date never comes, and the sexual confrontation is avoided. In the words of Ruth K., a magazine editor from Florida, "I'm good for about two dates. After that, the pressure starts to build, so I make myself scarce."

What is particularly unfortunate about this is that many relationships with tremendous potential never get a chance to develop. As Barbara B., a hospital administrator from New York, put it, "In a way I regret it, but if a guy doesn't impress me as being Mr. Right on the first date, I usually won't go out with him again. Maybe I could have had a few good relationships . . . or a brief fling or two . . . even a good friendship would be better than nothing. But it's too much trouble—this sexual-liberation thing makes everything too complicated."

At this point you may be thinking, "But I'm not like most men—I never pressure women into bed. Why do they stop dating *me?*" Unfortunately, it doesn't matter what you are like—women have become so sensitive to the dating timetable that they don't want to stick around long enough to find out your particular views on the subject. If you can't quickly convince a woman that you are very different from most of the men she has met (a difficult task, since she won't be giving you much time to do so), she will automatically assume that you expect to be sleeping with her after one or two dates, and she will react accordingly.

Of course, in this era of progressive sexuality, every woman isn't worried about the consequences of the dating timetable—some women have willingly integrated it into their lifestyles, and have no objection to sleeping with a man on the first date. But there is a catch—although these women may sleep with every man they date, they don't date every man who asks. In fact, these women won't give most men the time of day—they are extraordinarily particular about the men they date (far more particular than the many women troubled by the dating timetable). Therefore, although women's feelings about the dating timetable may vary, for men it is always a no-win situation.

The Dating Equation

Another concept which has made dating less appealing to women is the dating equation:

$$\$\$\$\ \text{INVESTED}♂ = \text{SEX OWED}♀$$

This equation implies that the more money a man spends on a woman, the more that woman is obligated to sleep with him. Now you may be saying to yourself, "That's ludicrous" (I *hope* you're saying this), but many men accept the validity of this equation without question.

If you find this hard to believe, you would be interested to hear about an experience I had recently while being interviewed on a talk show in Connecticut. To get the audience involved in the show, the host decided to ask them their opinion of the dating equation. By a show of hands (and a few cheers), *half* the audience indicated that they agreed with the principles of this equation. Even I was a little bit surprised to see how many people felt this way.

How has the dating equation affected women's behavior? For one thing, more and more women are now insisting they pay their own way on dates. True, some of these women are only asserting their independence, but many more are clearly demonstrating that they don't want to be sexually obligated. And rightfully so! A woman is not some sort of glorified vending machine—an object a man pumps money into expecting something in return (and wants to kick when nothing comes out)—a woman is a complex human being who wants to be treated as such. . . . DONT FORGET IT!

The dating equation has also made women more wary of men who shower them with gifts after only one or two dates, and men who insist upon taking them on high-priced, whirlwind evenings (unless, of course, the man asks the woman to pay half the bill at the end, but that can create other problems). Some women won't even go out with men who are known to spend excessive amounts of money on the first few dates. "After all," one woman remarked, "who knows what they'll want in return?"

Don't misunderstand me, I am not implying that women are attracted to cheap guys—they're not. But spending a lot of money does not always make the kind of impression you would like it to make.

More Causes for Concern

In addition to the dating timetable and dating equation, there are several other factors which are having a considerable influence on women's dating behavior:

COMMITMENT PRESSURE

Many women terminate the dating process very quickly when they are subjected to premature commitment pressure. (Is there such a thing as mature commitment pressure? Yes, but it doesn't come until a relationship has been well-developed.) Anna G., a real-estate broker from New York told me, "Most men *don't give you the chance* to get to know them. After a couple of dates, they start telling you how they don't want you to see any other people, how you're the most wonderful woman they've ever met, how they want you to meet their family . . . this is too much to handle after only one or two dates. I can't imagine what they would say after three or four." This woman, like many others I've spoken with, told me she is constantly cutting off relationships because she can't handle the pressure men put on her to make a commitment. She also emphasized that, "Men have to learn that a woman's desire to make a serious commitment doesn't develop overnight. If a man doesn't have any patience, he'll never have a successful relationship . . . at least not with any of the women I know." I couldn't have said it any better myself.

SUPERFICIALITY

"Sometimes you can go out with a guy five or six times and still know nothing about him—that's what I hate about dating," complained Catherine B., a nurse from Texas. We all know how dating tends to be extremely superficial. Everyone puts on their best face for the evening and acts out the role of "winer and diner" or "winee and dinee." Yet because we are trapped in these rigid roles, often our best, most natural qualities don't surface—even if we want them to.

But if your true personality does not show through and a woman doesn't get the chance to discover your best qualities, then you become just another boring dinner date. Once this happens, the likelihood of rejection increases dramatically, as illustrated by this comment from Mary L., a high-school math teacher from New York: "If a guy isn't comfortable enough with himself to just *be* himself, I get turned-off. Maybe some women like stiff, formal dates, but to me, there's nothing worse."

PERSONAL SAFETY

Women's fears and concerns do not magically disappear once they are outside the bar scene. Most women will admit that they often worry about their personal safety when they are considering whether or not to go on a date with a man (especially one they don't know very much about). As Sherri V., a computer saleswoman from California, explained, "It's amazing how insensitive most guys are to a woman's fears. They expect you to think nothing of getting into a car with a guy you hardly know and spending the entire evening at his mercy. Dating new guys used to scare me to death—I would smoke half a pack of cigarettes just waiting for my dates to arrive . . . and the other half during the date. Thank God I got married when I did. If I hadn't, my lungs would have been black by the time I was thirty."

Although you may find such fears to be totally irrational (you know you would never hurt a fly), to a woman, they are very real. The less a woman knows about you, the more these fears are apt to affect her decision to accept or not accept a date with you.

THE LIMITATIONS OF TIME AND ENERGY

For the working woman, the lack of free time has made dating even less appealing. Shauna C., a department store executive from Massachusetts, admitted, "My job gives me so little free time, the last thing I want to do is spend an entire evening on a date with some strange guy." Many women share this feeling. What could be worse then spending your precious free time worrying about things like sexual pressure and personal safety?

In addition, many working women find dating more exhausting than their jobs. Janice P., a lawyer from New Jersey, told me, "I can't date all the time—it takes too much energy. I have to worry about what I'm going to wear . . . I have to clean my apartment just in case he comes in . . . I like to relax when I'm not working—dating is *not* relaxing."

The Decline of Dating

Now you know why men are having so much trouble dating: women have too many good reasons to turn us down. Even if a woman is attracted to you, think of everything else she has to consider before accepting a date—the pressures, the problems, the fears. It's overwhelming. Therefore, it is not surprising that women are finding more pleasant, less pressured things to do with their valuable free time. More and more, I hear women say things such as, "I hardly date anymore," and, "I'm taking a break from dating." Some women have given up on dating entirely, including Cathy J., a free-lance writer from New York, who told me, "I don't care if I never have another date—dating is a pain in the ass."

Considering all the problems dating can bring, you

may find it surprising that *any* women are still willing to date. But most see no alternative—they feel that to have a relationship, they must play the dating game. Unfortunately, few of these women continue to have an easygoing attitude toward dating. Not only have they become incredibly particular about selecting dating prospects, but most remain extremely sensitive to the slightest sign of pressure or any other problems, ready to end everything at a moment's notice. As a result, even a man who passes the initial screening process can easily become a rejection statistic after one or two dates.

What is even more disconcerting is that men's problems with dating are likely to get much worse before they get better. As more and more women turn away from promiscuity in an effort to put meaning back into their relationships, dating—which is so hopelessly intertwined with sex—is becoming less and less appealing. Indeed, it may only be a matter of time before it is impossible for any man to develop a relationship by proceeding on a date-to-date basis.

What can men do? Is there any way to cultivate relationships without encountering all of these unpleasant pressures and problems? Yes there is, if you're willing to stop dating. But how can a man have a productive social life if he doesn't date? The truth is that any man can lay the foundation for a successful relationship *without ever going on a single date*—it all begins with two simple steps:

Step #1—A New Vocabulary.

Every time I hear a man use the word "date," I cringe.

Like "pick-up" and "score," the word date brings too many negative images to a woman's mind—eliminate it from your vocabulary (regardless of whether or not you're in the company of women). From now on you will be "spending time" with women, "getting together" with them, "meeting" them, "seeing" them—anything but dating them.

Step #2—A New Attitude.

A new vocabulary is not enough. If you treat today's woman the same way you always treated your dates, she will react to you accordingly, no matter what words you use. If you want to develop a successful relationship with women, you must also change your attitude. As I have said before, relationships do not develop on a fixed schedule. Each proceeds at a different rate, determined by circumstances unique to that relationship. Any attempt to push this natural developmental process forward will only discourage a woman's interest.

From now on, instead of forcing a woman to reject you before she knows anything about you (a decision brought on by the pressures of dating), you must give a woman plenty of time to get to know you without making her feel pressured to make any decisions. This means *you must establish friendship and trust first*, and leave romance for later. If you do, you will open the door to unlimited possibilities.

This may all sound terrific, but how do you start? Well, let's suppose you've just met a woman you think you're interested in (perhaps you met her at work, on a train, or through a mutual friend; whether you met by chance or through introduction, your course of action is never very different). Typically, men will rush to the phone and try to make a date; some men won't even wait that long—they'll press the woman for a date the moment they've met her. By now, however, you should understand why this type of behavior can mark the beginning of the end of a relationship. So what do you do instead?

To start building your relationship, while minimizing the likelihood of rejection, the first thing to do is look for ways for the two of you to get more well-acquainted that don't necessitate making any type of prearranged plans:

- If you see the woman often (at work, school, etc.), try to talk with her whenever you get an opportunity (of course, make sure you're not a nuisance).
- If you don't see her often, but you know where she works or where she spends her free time, drop by on occasion to say hello. If she's not around, or if she's busy, leave a brief note (no love notes, please)—she'll appreciate the gesture.

These little ice-breakers may sound silly, but they can make a big difference in the future of your relationship; they give a woman exactly what she needs—the chance to get to know more about you without feeling pressured (a chance she may never have had if you immediately tried to start wining and dining her). Just remember, these encounters should be kept free of romantic overtones; they are simply opportunities to make friendly conversation in order to get more well-acquainted—nothing more.

Of course, if you don't have the opportunity to get more well-acquainted via these low-key ice-breakers, you're going to have to make some type of prearranged meeting plans. In fact, even if you *do* have one, or several opportunities to break the ice, sooner or later it is going to be necessary to plan some type of get-together if a woman is to get to know you better. What should you do? Often, a good opportunity will present itself naturally, but if it doesn't, the smartest thing to do is to suggest a *simple, informal, low-pressure* get-together (for no more than an hour or two), such as meeting for lunch. This has several advantages:

She feels no pressure.

Asking a woman to meet you for lunch makes it very clear that all you want to do is talk—this eliminates any concern she may have about confronting sexual pressure; you would be amazed at how important this can be to her. In addition, since your expenses won't be excessive, she is not likely to feel the pressures of the dating equation.

No time problems.

Because women value their free time, meeting for lunch is ideal. Although a busy woman may neither be willing, nor able to spend five hours on a dinner date, she will often be willing and able to set aside an hour to meet you for lunch. After all, she has to eat anyway—why not have some company?

No fears.

Because you will be meeting in a public place, a woman has no reason to be overly concerned about her personal safety.

Better communication.

Two people can learn more about each other in one hour during a relaxed, informal lunch than they can in five hours during a formal, pressured dinner date. The more a woman can learn about you the first time you're together, the better the odds of there being a next time.

Rejection is minimized.

An invitation to lunch minimizes the risk of rejection by minimizing pressures, worries, and fears; just make sure your attitude is as low-key as the activity (when you ask her to meet you for lunch, don't sound like you're asking for her hand in marriage). If a woman won't meet you for lunch, there probably isn't anything she *will* meet you for.

Meeting for lunch clearly represents the type of circumstances that are ideal for giving a woman the chance to learn about you (and vice versa) without making her feel as though she is on a high-pressure date. But lunch is by no means your only option—any situation that is relaxed, low-pressured, nonthreatening, and not overly time-consuming is suitable for your first get-together. Other possibilities include meeting for coffee, meeting for a drink after work, playing tennis, or even going out for an ice-cream cone. Use your imagination, and if you can, give the woman a choice; just keep in mind the reasons behind the idea of meeting for lunch.

Slow, but Steady

Meeting for lunch is not a revolutionary concept; for many, it is standard procedure. But what's next? A night on the town? A quiet little evening at your place? Maybe a romantic weekend getaway? Wrong, wrong, and wrong.

Unfortunately, most men regard meeting for lunch as a never-to-be-repeated event. Once the roast beef sandwich is finished, they can't wait to dive head-first into the high-pressure dating muck. All too often, the results are predictably disastrous. Men don't seem to realize that "one lunch, does not a relationship make" (Shakespeare?). It usually takes a lot of time for two people to get to know each other, and shifting gears during the fragile first few weeks of a relationship (not to mention the first few days) may quickly destroy any progress you have made. Remember, most women are in no hurry to get involved. Putting pressure on at this point will only encourage a woman to reject you before she has had any chance to get to know you.

So what do you do, meet her for lunch once a week for the next twenty years? Certainly not, but the reasons I recommended meeting for lunch are not to be quickly forgotten. Until you sense a great degree of comfort and closeness between yourself and a woman—whether it takes three hours, three weeks, or three months—you must continue to make your get-togethers as relaxed, low-key, and nonpressured as possible.

Sure, you can meet for lunch or brunch a few more times—you can even meet for a *casual* dinner (let her know ahead of time that it won't end late)—but you have many other options. Pick up on her interests and try to do things you would both enjoy: go jogging, take in an exhibit, ask her to help you with your clothes shopping (she'll be flattered). Even better, try to take advantage of your special talents. Perhaps you're a golfer, a photographer, or a tournament bridge player. Offer to share your expertise; few women can resist the chance to learn something new which intrigues them. Besides, opportunities like this can be a great help to you because they show you off in your best light.

For example, a friend of mine (Don) once spent an afternoon teaching a woman he had just met (Vicki) to use her new camera. Vicki recently told me how that day marked the turning point in their relationship. She admitted that until that afternoon, she hadn't been particularly interested in Don, but that day she discovered, "He was so smart . . . and he had so much patience—I was really impressed." The two of us agreed that it would have taken Vicki at least ten dinner dates to find that out. We also agreed that Don wouldn't have lasted ten dates (the way Vicki spoke, he wouldn't have lasted two).

Another woman—Gail R., a travel consultant from Michigan—recalled that one of her most memorable relationships began when an old college acquaintance called her one day to invite her to go fishing. She told me, "If he had asked me to dinner, I never would have gone . . . but fishing seemed so harmless. Besides, I had never been fishing before, and I was curious." Although the fishing trip consisted of going out for a few hours in a rented rowboat, Gail remembered it as being one of the most enjoyable afternoons she had spent with a man in a long, long time.

Fishing, shopping, meeting for brunch . . . it doesn't matter what you do. If you can stick to this low-stress approach and resist trying to turn your friendly outings into steamy romantic interludes, your relationship should steadily improve. In other words, if you can stay away from pressure-packed dates, and resist attempting any manipulative seduction scenes, you will soon see how quickly a woman's feelings toward you can develop—feelings that never get a chance to surface if the pressure is on. You will also see how quickly your interest in a woman can grow—it's amazing how much you can learn about a woman, and how much you can enjoy her company, when your mind isn't preoccupied with figuring out ways to get her into bed by the end of the evening.

A SECOND OPTION: DATE LESS

I don't expect every man to feel immediately comfortable with the idea of never going on a date again. After all, old behavior patterns are hard to break. At the same time, however, you should now clearly understand why dating has been giving you so much difficulty, and you also probably realize that things will not improve until you make some changes.

If you are not ready to eliminate dating from your lifestyle, you should at least be willing to strike a compromise: Start depressurizing your dating patterns by interjecting some low-key get-togethers amidst your "big nights out." For example, if you go out for a night on the town this weekend, meet for a casual lunch the next time you go out. This will make things easier for you and easier for her, and will also help wean you away from your old dating behavior. In time, you will become more comfortable with this new style of social interaction, and then you will be able to free yourself from the wining and dining trap forever.

More Than Just Friends?

As your friendship/relationship slowly develops, you will have plenty of time to evaluate your feelings toward the woman, and she will also have time to evaluate her feelings toward you. Sometimes, it may become obvious that the two of you aren't that compatible, and you may choose to let the relationship dissolve. Other times, you may decide that you enjoy your friendship, but that you would rather not let it develop into something more serious. This is easily accomplished by simply maintaining the low-key friendly attitude you have been using thus far. If your feelings change later on, you can change the nature of the relationship later on—*as long as you maintain your friendship, there is no time limit.*

It is also possible that it may be the woman who is not ready for a more intimate relationship. Perhaps it is a bad time for her, perhaps she still feels she doesn't know you well enough, or maybe she is just afraid of making a commitment—whatever her reasons may be, she will probably be sending out signals to let you know she isn't looking, or isn't ready for anything serious. If this is how she feels, do not try to pressure her into changing her mind—you will only turn her off. Instead, continue to see her in the same low-key fashion. This will give her feelings toward you more time to develop, and at the same time, it will leave the door open for something more meaningful in the future.

But what if you have a strong interest in the woman, and you sense she has developed a more-than-friendly interest in you? If this is the case, you are now ready to *slowly* let your get-togethers become less casual and more intimate. Just don't push it (no confessions of undying love, please!)—if you pressure her now, you could still ruin everything.

"New Woman"

As the tone of your relationship begins to change, it may not be long before you begin noticing changes in the woman's attitude and body language which indicate her growing desire to sleep with you. But before you take her by the hand and lead her into the bedroom, you'd better ask yourself one question: Are you ready?

6

The Bedroom Blues

WOMEN have most of their difficulties with sexual pressure *outside* the bedroom. Men, however, have the opposite problem, for although we anxiously await the moment that a new relationship is consummated in the bedroom, many of us are finding that this moment marks the beginning of a whole new set of problems—problems brought on by the "pressure to perform."

The pressure to perform is, in part, due to traditional patterns of sexual interaction which place the burden of initiation and success on the shoulders of the male. But even if a fair share of this responsibility were to be assumed by the woman—as it sometimes is—men would still be subject to significant problems. This is because of the limitations of our anatomy—a man can fake a lot of things, but an erection is not one of them.

Does this mean that men are forever to be plagued by

sexual pressure when they step foot into the bedroom? Not necessarily—sexual pressure *can* be significantly reduced, or even eliminated, if you are willing to follow certain suggestions:

Taking the Pressure Off

You don't have to work at Masters' and Johnson's to know that great sex is a rarity the first time two people sleep together. In the beginning, sex is usually a lot more work than pleasure; no two women are exactly the same, and it often takes a fair amount of time to become acclimated to a new partner's particular sexual needs. If you are troubled by sexual pressure, and wish to minimize the likelihood of encountering any problems during this adjustment period, it is important that the following elements have been established in your relationship:

- Friendship
- Trust
- Communication
- Caring
- Comfort
- Genuine attraction

If any, or all, of these are missing, sexual pressure may quickly build, and your "first time" may also be your last. To insure the presence of these elements, it is necessary to take certain precautions (no jokes, please) before you ever get to the bedroom:

BE SELECTIVE

Why is it that no matter how we worry about sexual pressure, we never seem to be able to pass up an opportunity to jump into bed with the first woman who makes herself available? Are we slaves to our sexual desires? Seemingly so, but this creates a rather unpleasant paradox, for the penis which coaxes us into the bedroom is the same penis which shuts down once inside. Why does this happen? Because once we are under the covers, the penis becomes a painfully accurate barometer of our feelings, and if we are not genuinely attracted to, interested in, and comfortable with the woman we are sleeping with, it shows via some form of sexual dysfunction.

There is only one remedy for this. If you are troubled by the pressure to perform, you must become far more discriminating in your selection of bed partners, even if you have to struggle through some celibate periods. Failure to do so will only leave you to be haunted by fears of performance problems.

YOU ARE NOT A SEX OBJECT—DON'T ACT LIKE ONE

There is something about the image of a tennis pro that attracts women who are searching for sexual satisfaction, and *only* sexual satisfaction (although these women are a small minority, they do exist). These women usually place an abnormally large amount of emphasis on a man's sexual skills, and they are not apt to be very understanding if his performance is not up to their expectations. For tennis pros, this problem comes with the territory (they knew the job was dangerous when they took it), but there are many other men who suffer from "tennis pro syndrome." These men make every effort to project the same image that is the tennis pro's curse—that of the stud who is capable of satisfying any and all women (their most common remark being some variation of, "You haven't experienced anything till you've slept with me"). This attitude only welcomes problems.

If you want women to stop treating you like a sex object, you must first stop treating yourself like one. After all, the last thing you want to do is sleep with a woman who is only attracted to you because she thinks you're a superhuman bedroom athlete—sooner or later, she's bound to be disappointed.

STOP RUSHING

Rushing into the bedroom is not only likely to turn a woman off, but it can turn you off as well. As I said before, you are least prone to being affected by sexual pressure if there is trust, communication, comfort, caring, interest, friendship, and genuine attraction in a relationship. But *these essential elements do not develop overnight*—some may not develop for weeks or months (or they may never develop)—and ignoring their absence only invites sexual pressures and problems. Our sexual behavior patterns suggest we are thoroughly insensitive to this. For example, in the "Singles" study conducted by Simenauer and Carroll, almost two thirds of the men surveyed indicated they usually sleep with a woman on the first to third date. This can be a big mistake. In addition, this same study revealed that women were four times more likely than men to feel that it can take months before they are emotionally ready to sleep with someone. This is also bad news.

If you want to stop worrying about sexual pressure, start making it a habit not to sleep with a woman the first few times you are together. If your interest in her is genuine, and she is interested in you as well, you will have many other opportunities later on—why risk getting off to a bad start?

But if the first few times are off limits, when *should* you start sleeping with a woman?—the fourth time you are with her? . . . the fifth time? . . . after you've been seeing her for ten years? There is no *one* right answer to this question—every situation is unique—therefore, the proper timing in that situation is also unique. But there is one rule of thumb which will help you decide whether or not you are ready: you are ready when you sense a reasonable degree of comfort, caring, communication, trust, friendship, and attraction between yourself and the woman—whether it takes a few days, several weeks, or many months. It's that simple.

NO ONE-NIGHT STANDS

A man in one of my seminars approached me before class to discuss something which had been bothering him terribly. The last three times he had gone home with a woman he met in a bar, he found himself experiencing sexual difficulties. He asked me what he could do about it, so I told him not to go home with any woman he met in a bar. Although he thought I was being obnoxious, by the end of the class, he understood what I meant; as I mentioned earlier, there is nothing worse than a one-night stand—it is the embodiment of everything a man concerned about sexual pressure should avoid. By now you should understand why this is so:

- Your failure to be selective (obviously you are not being very selective if you don't care to be with the woman for more than one night) encourages the possibility that your true feelings will betray you in bed by manifesting themselves as some sort of sexual dysfunction (remember, inside the bedroom your penis is usually a lot more honest than you are).
- During a typical one-night stand, the woman knows so little about you that it is hard for her to view you as something more than a sex object. Besides, even if she *isn't* critically evaluating your skill as a lover, your fear that she *is* can be just as debilitating.
- The logistics of the one-night stand leave no opportunity for the "six essential elements" to develop before

curtain time. This not only makes it more likely that something will go wrong, but also insures that if something *does* go wrong, the problem will be blown way out of proportion.

Add to this the risk of disease, and the fact that one bad sexual experience—by badly shaking your confidence—can lead to other similar experiences, and it becomes very obvious that one-night stands are just not worth the risk.

Learning How to Say "No"

Now that you know why and when you should be turning down certain tempting sexual opportunities, it is time to learn how. But is this really anything to worry about? After all, men always initiate sex, so if you don't think you should be sleeping with a woman, all you have to do is refrain from initiating anything, right? Wrong! Women may not feel comfortable picking up a strange man on the street or calling a man for a date, but women are not so shy once they are with a man behind closed doors. In fact, a substantial percentage of women feel very comfortable initiating sex, and many more are not embarrassed to clearly indicate their interest through the use of body language.

Therefore, if you want to avoid some very awkward moments, you are going to have to learn the various ways of telling a woman "no" in a manner which won't offend or insult her. Although this sounds as though it will be difficult to learn, it may not be as hard as you think. After all, you should already be familiar with many of these techniques—women have been using them on you for years. The two approaches I recommend are as follows:

BY WORDS

If a woman comes on strong and you choose to resist her advances, she will probably wonder why and may even ask. It would help if you gave her an explanation, and in this case, honesty is usually the best policy. Tell her the truth: you're just not ready. If her interest in you is sincere, she may be disappointed, and she'll probably be very surprised, but she won't be turned off (if her interest in you was just a passing fancy, you are better off not having slept with her anyway). If you find this hard to believe, you might be interested to hear what happened to a good friend of mine who recently told a woman "no" using this straightforward approach.

After going through a series of short, disappointing sexual relationships, my friend Alan met and started seeing a woman who was an absolute knock-out. You can imagine how surprised this perfect "10" was when, at the end of their second evening together, Alan turned down her invitation to spend the night at her apartment. Immediately feeling he owed her an explanation, Alan told her the truth—he explained how he had just gone through a string of casual affairs which had left him disappointed and depressed. This time, he wanted to wait for a while—he wanted to get to know her better. This way, if at some later point they did sleep together, maybe it would be something a little more meaningful than what he had been experiencing recently.

How did the woman react to this explanation? "At first," Alan recalled, "she looked at me like I was nuts . . . and looking at her, I was beginning to think I was. But then a big smile broke out on her face, and she told me that was one of the nicest things a man had ever said to her." Did his approach really help? Well, he has been seeing her for over a year—I'll let you draw your own conclusion.

Although this honest approach is usually the best, there may be times when you are embarrassed to admit how you feel, or afraid that the truth might hurt the woman's feelings. In this case, it isn't terrible if you tell a little white lie to get you out of your predicament. Just don't make a habit of it—the repeated use of excuses may lead the woman to conclude that you're not too interested in her, and this will ultimately turn her off.

BY DEEDS

Many men would probably prefer not to have to give any explanation why they aren't ready to accept a woman's sexual advances. If this is how you feel, I recommend you play it safe until you feel ready to follow these suggestions:

Take advantage of safe situations.

If you are unsure whether or not you are ready, it is

wise to restrict your activities to situations which preclude any possibility of sexual entanglement—situations which, in effect, say "no" for you. Most daytime get-togethers and get-togethers with built-in time restrictions will serve your purposes very nicely (the same types of get-togethers you've been using to keep the pressure off *her*).

Control yourself.

The likelihood of a woman coming on to you is greatly affected by the way you handle the relationship and the way you handle yourself. If you are not ready for sexual intimacy, don't let your tone, or the tone of your relationship, suggest otherwise. Sending out mixed signals can easily confuse a woman, and it can even turn her off if she interprets it as a lack of sexual confidence.

Don't change gears until you *are ready.*

You are not operating on any timetable; don't let a woman (or your peers) pressure you to move the relationship forward if you are not ready to do so—rushing will only lead to problems.

By words or by deeds, the choice is yours. Just make sure you don't say "yes" until you feel you are ready, willing, and able.

Keeping the Pressure Off

Now that you see how you can alleviate the burden of sexual pressure by following my suggestions *outside* the bedroom, it is time to discuss how you can *keep* the pressure off once you are *inside* the bedroom—because sooner or later, you *will* be inside the bedroom.

To keep the pressure off, you must first make every effort to become a better lover. Since you now know what really makes a man "good in bed" (see Chapter 4), you should use this information to your best advantage. In addition, it is important to become aware of six sore spots that tend to cause trouble in the bedroom:

SORE SPOT #1—THE DECEPTIVE BIG "O"

Many men have been led to conclude that there is no point in focusing on things such as caring, closeness, and tenderness since women seem to be far more concerned with their orgasms than with anything else. These men have little difficulty supporting their argument—with so many women's magazines constantly running feature stories on the Big "O," it has to be pretty important.

But there is one flaw in this line of reasoning, for without the supports of things such as communication and tenderness, most women are unable to achieve orgasm with a man—it simply does not occur in an emotional void. Therefore, although a woman's orgasm *is* important, it is usually dependent on something far more important: a man's emotional performance.

SORE SPOT #2—ABUSE OF THE CLITORIS

"Once men discovered the clitoris, they forgot about everything else," a woman recently complained to me. This is not an isolated opinion—many women are angry that the publicity surrounding the clitoris has made it the focus of men's attention. Why are they upset?

- Because any man who makes a bee-line for the clitoris has probably ignored the far more important aspects of sexual intimacy.
- Because the clitoris is a highly sensitive organ, and overstimulation can be unpleasant, if not painful. How much stimulation is too much? That depends on the woman. How do you find out? Communication.

SORE SPOT#3—NOT ENOUGH FOREPLAY

Something else men tend to ignore is the importance of foreplay. How much foreplay does a woman require? Although some say they are satisfied with only a few minutes, many more insist they need much more time. In fact, most studies indicate that the majority of women prefer foreplay to last at least half an hour, if not longer. This should make it very clear that most women are *not* looking for a quick roll in the hay. This is a male fantasy which ignores what a woman really needs if she is to experience complete sexual fulfillment.

SORE SPOT #4—BY-THE-BOOK SEX

As I have mentioned several times, women are turned off by technical experts who ignore other, more important aspects of sexual intimacy. Mechanical, by-the-book sex *feels* like mechanical, by-the-book sex, and women don't like it—it makes them feel as though any other woman could easily take their place in your bed. *Make love to the woman you are in bed with*, not to the hypothetical female you read about in various "plumbing" manuals.

SORE SPOT #5—". . . BUT YOU NEVER ASKED"

A quick way to permanently turn a woman off is to ignore the issue of contraception. As one woman put it, "If a man cares, he asks." If you are unsure whether or not a woman is using any contraception, either ask her or use your own. This will not only let her know you care, but it will also save her, and you, from a lot of unnecessary trauma later on.

SORE SPOT #6—"WHAM, BAM, THANK YOU MA'AM"

Once you feel sexually satisfied, do you find yourself grabbing your coat and racing for the door or rolling over in bed and nodding off? If you're guilty of either of these two behavior patterns, chances are that a lot of women have not invited you back into their bedrooms. Many women consider the fifteen or twenty minutes after intercourse and/or orgasm to be the true test of whether or not a man is a good lover. A good lover does *not* doze off (unless his partner has dozed off), nor does he run out to catch the next train home. Quite the contrary, a good lover knows that his partner's and/or his orgasm does not mark the end of the evening, and he also knows that the time spent cuddling and talking afterward is just as important as intercourse itself.

Of course, this doesn't mean that you must stay with a woman until the next morning—she may feel you are taking advantage of her hospitality—but it does mean that you cannot turn off your attentiveness as soon as you are sexually satisfied. If you find yourself unable to stay turned on, something is probably lacking in your relationship, and you shouldn't be sleeping with her in the first place.

The Morning After

It's eight o'clock in the morning and the sunlight is pouring into the room through the windows. As you slowly open your eyes, you feel disoriented. Then you remember that you're not in your own bed. You turn to look at the figure sleeping beside you—if she is awake, she doesn't want you to know it. Trying not to disturb her, you carefully pull yourself out of bed. After a lengthy search for the various articles of clothing you had worn the night before, all items are finally accounted for. You take another look toward the bed . . . still no movement.

Now what? Do you wake her? Better not, she probably wants to sleep. Should you leave a note? Good idea . . . but you can't find a pen. Besides, what would you write? Maybe you should just call her later on . . . but what if she gets upset because you're not there when she wakes up? On the other hand, she may be glad you're not there. Well, you can't stay in her apartment the entire day waiting for her to get up. . . . What should you do?

Another familiar scenario? You have probably discovered that if you spend the night with a woman, the morning after, especially the first morning after, is a morning fraught with confusion and mixed emotions where an inability to handle yourself properly can turn a woman off for good. What *does* a woman expect from you the morning after? That depends on how long it took for the two of you to get to the bedroom.

IF YOU RUSHED

If your encounter was the result of a one-night stand, the woman may want to have absolutely nothing to do with the body she wakes up next to in the morning. How do you know if she wants you to leave as quickly as possible, or if she wants to spend the entire morning in your arms? You don't. How do you find out? You could try holding her in your arms when she wakes up, but if she screams as soon as she feels the touch of your hand, you may have to conclude that she has other things on her mind that morning (or she has very sensitive skin). On the other hand, if you ignore her in the morning and leave as soon as you can find your socks, it is very possible that you are leaving behind one very angry and insulted woman.

Is there any way to tell what a woman expects under these circumstances? Not unless she is very communicative. So what to you do? *Don't rush!*

IF YOU WAITED

Let's now suppose that, seeing the wisdom in my suggestions, you decided not to rush into the bedroom. Will this change the way a woman views the morning after? Absolutely. By treating sexual intimacy less casually, you have turned the morning after into something far more important for both of you. Now, instead of viewing it as a time of awkwardness and ill-feelings, it can be viewed as an extension of the night before—a time to talk, cuddle, perhaps even make love again. The *last* thing you should do under these circumstances is disappear as soon as you wake up. This is almost guaranteed to insult the woman you are with (quite unlike the one-night stand, where you might have been doing her a favor by disappearing).

But I must remind you here that even though everything seems warm and rosy on the first morning after:

• Just because you've slept with a woman once, it doesn't mean she is madly in love with you—she probably isn't.

• Just because you've slept with a woman once, it doesn't mean she wants to be with you during every free moment she has for the next ten years—she doesn't. No woman wants to be smothered.

• Just because you've slept with a woman once, it doesn't mean that the relationship is firmly established—it probably isn't. Although sex does help solidify a relationship, sex alone is not enough.

• If you've slept with a woman once, it *does* mean that she has a sincere interest in you—an interest which can be developed into a strong relationship if you continue to let things move *slowly* forward without pressuring her to make a commitment.

All of this information may not be that difficult for you to understand and accept, but it does leave one disturbing question unanswered: if sexual intimacy can no longer solidify a relationship, what can?

7

Where Do You Stand?

PERHAPS the most bothersome aspect of the modern relationship is that it seems to lack any reasonable degree of predictability. Instead of following the neat little paths which were so commonplace a few decades ago, relationships tend to move through peaks and troughs in much the same fashion as a volatile issue on the stock exchange—those that appear to be perfect one day are over the next, while others which seem destined to fail suddenly show dramatic improvement. Such volatility has put most of us in the dark as to where we stand in our relationships.

A substantial part of the male dilemma seems to be tied directly to the changes in women's attitudes toward sexual intimacy. Years of conditioning have made it difficult for us to accept that sex no longer works like some sort of magical, indestructible relationship glue, yet failure to acknowledge this only welcomes heartbreak. At the same time, even if we do accept the changing role of sexual intimacy, much confusion still remains. For if intimacy is not a reasonable indicator of the status of a relationship, what is?

Knowing Where You Stand

Although it is no longer easy for any man to determine exactly where he stands in a relationship, there are several indicators which can still help you make a reasonably accurate assessment of your situation—an assessment which will help you avoid making any gross overassumptions which can later lead to serious disappointments:

ARE THE "SIX ESSENTIAL ELEMENTS" PRESENT?

At the base of a good relationship, there is friendship, trust, communication, caring, comfort, and genuine attraction. Are any, or most of these elements missing from your relationship (on your part, *or* on hers)? If they are, it is probably not a very strong one. On the other hand, if all of these elements are present, your relationship has great potential, perhaps unlimited potential, provided you avoid the pitfalls discussed later in this chapter.

DID YOU RUSH INTO THE BEDROOM?

Relationships which are built upon a foundation of sexual intimacy, instead of such things as trust and communication, tend to be highly unstable and prone to collapse as soon as the sexual magic wears thin. Furthermore, the sooner sex enters into a relationship, the less you can use such intimacy as a measure of the degree to which you are involved. This is not to say that the sex is unimportant to a woman who immediately starts sleeping with you, it is only to say that it is usually difficult to judge *how* important it is. Since she is not likely to tell you in any direct fashion, and since you may fear the ramifications of asking her ("If I say something, will she get turned off because she thinks I'm taking this too seriously? Will she get turned off because she thinks I'm not taking this seriously enough?), you may find yourself trapped in the uneasy position of having no clue as to the status of your relationship.

"Decasualizing" sex, on the other hand, heightens its import—if you don't rush into the bedroom, sexual intimacy becomes a far more significant statement of your and her affection when you finally get there. Although such delayed intimacy offers no guarantees, and certainly does not entitle you to assume that any woman who sleeps with you under these conditions must be madly in love with you, it *does* entitle you to assume that the woman you are sleeping with views your relationship as much more than a casual fling. How much more? Time will tell—the relationship still has a long way to go—but in the meantime, you can comfort yourself with the knowledge that your "no rush" approach to intimacy has maximized the potential for future relationship growth.

WHAT DOES SHE SAY OR INTIMATE?

Often a woman will say or intimate certain things which make her feelings about your relationship very obvious (provided you are paying attention). She may talk about her need to avoid the temptations of settling down at this point in her life, how glad she was to get out of her last relationship because it was so serious, or something similar. You cannot afford to ignore these comments—they are being directed at you. If a woman talks vaguely about her need to avoid the temptations of settling into something serious, she is really saying, "Hey you—I'm not ready for something serious. Let's take it nice and slow for a while—I'll let you know when I'm ready for more."

Some women prefer to camouflage their sentiments even more. A man in one of my seminars told me how he had lived with a woman who used the experiences of a fictitious couple to vent her feelings about her relationship with him. It seems that every week she would have a new story about "Ron and Ellen"—one week Ron and Ellen were fighting because Ron expected too much too soon, the next week they were fighting because Ron was taking the relationship too seriously. Although this man believed in the existence of Ron and Ellen, he was still smart *enough* to pick up on the underlying messages in his girlfriend's stories, and change his attitude accordingly.

Although not many women go to the extreme of creating a fictitious couple to help solve their problems and get their points across, many women *will* discuss the good and bad aspects of other real relationships (and perhaps, exaggerate some of these aspects) in order to let you know how they feel about their relationship with you. Pay attention to these stories—they will help save your relationship from going down the drain unnecessarily.

HOW DO YOU FEEL?

If you sense there is something wrong with your relationship, you are probably right (unless you are terribly oversensitive)—consciously, or subsconciously, you are picking up signals from the woman you are involved with. The recent experience one friend of mine (Peter) had with his girlfriend (Cheryl) clearly illustrates this point:

It seems that after seeing Cheryl for almost six months, Peter was still feeling uneasy about Cheryl's attitude toward the relationship. Although Peter was having difficulty pinpointing which of Cheryl's actions were disturbing him, he continued to feel that something wasn't right. Every time he tried to discuss this with her, she would immediately reassure him that everything was fine, and that she just had a lot of things on her mind. But Peter was not comforted by her vague explanations. Finally, convinced that the situation was getting progressively worse, he decided to speak to me about it. After a lengthy discussion, the two of us came to the conclusion that Peter's attitudes—especially his constant displays of jealousy—might be impeding the progress of the relationship. No sooner did Peter make an effort to control his feelings of jealousy, than did Cheryl's behavior begin to improve.

If you experience similar feelings of uneasiness in a relationship, don't ignore them—they are often an early warning sign that the relationship may be in jeopardy. Instead, use them as an impetus to examine your behavior in light of the information presented in this book . . . before it's too late.

IS SHE SEEING OTHER MEN?

Just because a woman is seeing you on a steady basis, it does not necessarily mean she wishes to see you exclusively. There are several possible reasons for this:

She may fear losing her independence.

Many women are afraid of being trapped in a relationship—even if it is with a man they care for a great deal (I'm sure many of you can relate to this). As a way of reassuring themselves that they can maintain their independence, these women may continue to see other men, even if it's only on a very infrequent, casual basis.

Although these other relationships may be very superficial, they can be terribly bothersome to you. Still, any attempt to force a woman to stop seeing other men can be interpreted as an attempt to take away her independence. The way to encourage this type of woman to stop seeing other men is not by issuing ultimatums, but instead, by convincing her that you respect her need to maintain her independence within the framework of a relationship—even if it's a very serious relationship.

She may be protecting her feelings.

Sometimes a woman will refuse to see one man exclusively because she is afraid of putting herself in an emotionally vulnerable position. Typically, a woman who feels this way has had a bad experience with a long-term relationship, and is wary of such relationships and of men in general. Such a woman will often resist getting involved in another monogamous relationship until an inordinate amount of trust has been established between herself and the man she is interested in. This, of course, takes a lot of time.

She may be unsure.

Just because you feel very strongly about a woman, it does not necessarily guarantee that her feelings toward you are equally as strong. As I mentioned earlier, such a disparity in feelings is very common when a relationship is in its infancy, and until a woman has had ample time for her feelings to develop, she may not wish to restrict her social activities to just one man.

If your relationship is relatively new, this type of behavior should not be interpreted as a sign of a woman's permanent lack of interest—it is far more likely that she just needs more time for her interest to develop. If you try to force a resolution at this point, you may find yourself being handed your walking papers, but if you are patient, the situation will often be rectified in time as the woman's feelings toward you slowly strengthen.

She may not be that *interested.*

Just as you may sometimes have a limited interest in a woman, the reverse is also possible—a woman may enjoy spending time with you, and may even sleep with you occasionally, but she may not wish to see you exclusively. Under these circumstances, the passage of time may not significantly change the woman's attitude (at least, not for the better).

The one saving grace of this type of situation is that a woman who feels this way will usually make her feelings very clear to you. This leaves it up to you to decide whether or not the positive aspects of remaining involved outweigh the negative ones.

If you decide to continue to be involved in such a relationship, it would be wise for you to widen your social sphere—this will make you less prone to getting badly hurt later on. Although it is possible for this type of situation to improve dramatically over time, you'll fare better with a more practical assessment of the situation (and if it does improve, so much the better).

IS SHE SLEEPING WITH OTHER MEN?

If a woman is sleeping with other men, she is making a very obvious statement about the status of your relationship. As I discussed earlier, the vast majority of women find it difficult or impossible to be meaningfully and sexually involved with more than one man at a time. So unless the woman you're seeing is a member of the small minority who don't feel this way, she probably doesn't consider your relationship to be that meaningful—at least, not yet.

In time, this dilemma should resolve itself one way or the other. But if you are hoping for a positive resolution—namely, that the woman's feelings toward you will be strengthened to the point where she will want to stop sleeping with other men—do not issue any premature ultimatums. Even if a woman cares about you a great deal, trying to force her decision will only push her in the wrong direction—especially since she has someone else to turn to if she turns away from you. Is there anything you *can* do to encourage a positive resolution? Absolutely:

Keep the pressure off.

Give her time to come to terms with her ambivalence. The less you pressure her, the more likely she is to ultimately decide in your favor.

Keep your options open.

Don't limit your social activities if she isn't limiting hers. The presence of other women can give you a healthier outlook on the situation, and provide her with a new perspective as well.

What if, after following these suggestions, the situation remains unresolved? If a reasonable amount of time has passed (and I don't consider two weeks reasonable), and you are still unhappy with the way things stand, it is *you* who must now make some decisions. Does it look as though things are improving, or do you feel trapped in a no-win situation? If you think it's no-win, it is probably wise to spare yourself from any further aggravation and bail out at this point.

If, however, the situation seems to have promise, keep the pressure off and continue to let your relationship slowly build. At the same time, you may wish to decide how long you can go on sharing the woman's affections with another man. If this period of time elapses and there is still no major change in the relationship, then, and only then, is it reasonable to issue an honest ultimatum.

Problems and Pitfalls

Even if all the signs are right and your relationship appears to be steadily improving, you can never afford to be too smug—many problems may still lie ahead of you, and the inability to avoid or overcome the more serious ones can ruin even the best relationship. Although these problems are far too numerous and relationship-specific to be listed in any book, most can be avoided or solved by exercising good judgment in conjunction with your newly enlightened attitude. There are five pitfalls, however, which are so common to our relationships with the "new woman," yet potentially so dangerous, that they merit discussion here:

PITFALL #1—TAKING THE RELATIONSHIP FOR GRANTED

A man in one of my seminars told me an unpleasant story about his most recent relationship. He had been living with a woman for almost six months when one day, he came home to an empty apartment—she was gone, her clothes were gone, and all that was left was a note which said, "I'm surprised you even looked for a note—I didn't think you'd realize I was gone." What disturbed me most about this story was that this man not only insisted he loved the woman, but also insisted he hadn't done anything wrong.

Although this man was sure he hadn't done anything wrong, his problem was that *he hadn't done anything at all*—he had let himself be lulled into complacency by a false sense of security. As most women will be more than happy to remind you, if a relationship does not continue to move forward, it dies. Men tend to ignore this, believing instead that nothing can go wrong with a relationship once it has been established. This is, of course, untrue. *No relationship can ever be taken for granted*—you can't even take marriage for granted (as the current divorce statistics make so plain). Maintaining a strong relationship is an active process which demands constant communication and a concerted effort on everyone's behalf. If a woman senses you are neglecting the relationship, she may start looking for someone else who won't. Relationships take work!

PITFALL #2—OVERKILL

Regardless of how well your relationship is developing, you must never make the mistake of trying to smother a woman (this holds true even if your relationship is long passed the solidifying stage). You will be hard-pressed to find any woman who wants to spend every single moment of her free time with you; spending this much time together just isn't healthy for a relationship, and overfamiliarity can breed contempt.

If a woman says she needs a few hours or a few days to herself (or even f she wants to take a vacation without you), don't argue with her—it doesn't mean she is losing interest, it only means she is smart enough to realize how important it is for each of you to have time to yourselves. Failure to recognize the importance of this need for breathing space can be disastrous for a relationship, especially since a woman will view your attempts to smother her as both a sign of your insecurity and a threat to her independence. These are two very serious offenses in the mind of the new woman.

There is a corollary to this point: it is a serious mistake to cut off all other friends and outside interests once you've become involved in a relationship. How many of your friends mysteriously disappear every time they get involved with a woman, only to apologetically reappear a few months later with a new hard-luck story? Do you do this to them also? Well, perhaps your relationships wouldn't end so quickly if you realized how unhealthy this is. Cutting yourself off from friends and interests makes you too dependent on one human being. This kind of dependency can be an uncomfortable burden on the shoulders of an independent woman who wants and needs time to herself. In addition, if and when the relationship does end, you may find yourself with no one to turn to for support—some friends are not very sympathetic after they have been abandoned one too many times.

PITFALL #3—SPACE-INVADING

I recently interviewed a man (Robert) who shared the following story with me:

Robert had been living in the suburbs of New York City, but worked in Manhattan. This made it necessary for him to go through the pains of a daily commute. But then something happened to him—he met and started seeing Nina, a woman who lived a few blocks away from his office in Manhattan. As the relationship developed, Robert found it easier to stay overnight at Nina's place two or three times a week than to return home at the end of a late evening with her. The way he saw it, he had the best of both worlds—he was able to see Nina often, and he was also able to save a lot of the time, energy, and money he had been wasting on the train five days a week.

After a while, Robert moved a few of his basics into Nina's apartment (a couple of suits, some shirts, shoes, some casual clothing, etc.); he said that she seemed not to mind. He was wrong. One day, after several months had gone by, Robert arrived at Nina's apartment to find his basics, neatly packed into several shopping bags, waiting for him at the front door. He was shocked, but he shouldn't have been—after all, he had become a space-invader.

Many men find it very easy to make this type of half-move into a woman's apartment. They figure that if they're going to be sleeping there several nights a week, they might as well move some items in to make their stay more pleasant. But this can be a *big* mistake; even if the woman doesn't voice an objection, your invasion of her personal living space can turn her off *fast*—especially since she is paying all of the bills. *Independent women don't like space-invaders.* (Of course, if a woman *asks* you to move in, it's a very different story—we'll discuss this in the next chapter.)

PITFALL #4—THE "OPEN RELATIONSHIP"

One of the easiest ways to jeopardize your relationship is by ascribing to the having-your-cake-and-eating-it-too philosophy behind the "open relationship." Any man who is concerned about the problem of sexual pressure should run the other way every time he hears the words, "open relationship"; the last thing you want to do is to place yourself in a situation which invites a direct comparison of your sexual performance to the performance of another man (even if a woman does not *want* to compare—as most don't—it is hard not to under these circumstances). Such comparisons, or even the fear of such comparisons, can have a devastating effect on your ego and on your relationship, as illustrated by the experience of George M., a man I recently interviewed:

George told me he had always been petrified of making a commitment to a woman, and thought he could solve all his problems by coercing his girlfriend Lisa into agreeing to have an open relationship. "It is the mature thing to do," he told her, "it will give us both our necessary space." After a few weeks of being subjected to this sales pitch, Lisa reluctantly agreed.

For the next few months, everything was fine, but then Lisa dropped a bomb—she told George she had met another man. She didn't expect George to mind very much; in fact, she probably thought he would be happy to hear it. He wasn't . . . he was mortified. For the next two weeks, George was unable to make love to her, and shortly thereafter, Lisa left him for the other man.

This story brings out a second drawback of the open relationship. As I have stressed previously, most women cannot, and do not want to be meaningfully and intimately involved with more than one man at the same time. If you push a woman into an open relationship, you may be pushing her into the arms of another man who is very happy to be with her, and her *alone*.

Another man I interviewed, Eric K., also had a story to tell about the difficulties of the open relationship. For almost eight months, Eric had successfully managed to stay involved in two relationships simultaneously, one in town and one out-of-town. Eventually, however, his in-town sweetheart got fed up—she felt their relationship had developed to the point where Eric should be willing to abandon his weekend trips to sweetheart number two.

But Eric felt very comfortable having two affairs, and he was afraid of closing himself off socially by committing himself to only one woman. Seeing that Eric was not willing to close up the open relationship, the in-town girlfriend got disgusted, and finally handed him his walking papers. Depressed and badly shaken, Eric turned to his out-of-town girlfriend for support. But it seems that he leaned on her so heavily that she got turned off, and left him less than a month later.

Both of these stories illustrate that you should not be fooled by the surface appeal of the open relationship—invariably, it is the man who ends up suffering the most from this type of arrangement.

PITFALL #5—REVERTING TO OLD ROLES.

A year ago, two friends of mine, Richard and Anne, got married after living together for nearly three years. All the time they had lived together, Richard and Anne had an unusually strong relationship; they were an ideal example of how two independent people could still interact successfully in the framework of a meaningful relationship.

After not having heard from the couple for many months,

I finally received a telephone call from Richard. He called to tell me that his marriage was on the brink of divorce. I was shocked; I couldn't understand how everything could have deteriorated so severely within such a short period of time. But then I heard Richard's story. It seems that after he got married, he decided that he didn't want his marriage to be just a continuation of the original living-together arrangement. Instead, he wanted a traditional marriage—a family, a house, and a wife devoted to taking care of both (upon hearing this, I cringed, knowing what was to follow). Anne, on the other hand, had other ideas; she was a very successful attorney who loved her work, and had absolutely no intention of giving it up at this point in her life. Clearly, she had no interest in becoming a housewife.

Once these differences were openly discussed, the perfect relationship came apart at the seams. By the time Richard called me, he and Anne were barely on speaking terms. "What can I do?" he pleaded. "How can I make her change?" I told Richard the truth—he couldn't *make* her do anything. If Anne was to change her ideas about marriage, it would have to be her decision—and frankly, I didn't expect this would be happening in the foreseeable future.

I wondered why Richard hadn't discussed his traditional views with Anne before he got married. When I asked him about this, he told me, "At the time, I wasn't really sure. And besides, I was afraid of turning her off. I figured that once we were married, it would be easier to convince her to change." I then explained to him that the reason his relationship had been so successful for all of those years was because he never tried to make her change, but instead, had been totally respectful of who she was and what she was doing with her life. In the past year, he had undone all that he had accomplished prior to that.

The couple are presently seeing a marriage counselor, but I don't expect this to do much good. At least not unless Richard drastically changes his expectations and learns to once again accept Anne for what she is . . . an independent woman, not a domesticated housekeeper.

I have chosen to use this story in order to show how detrimental *any* attempt to revert back to traditional roles can be to a relationship—even one which has long since passed through the solidifying phase. Whether you've been seeing a woman for six weeks or six years, you can never try to revert back to behavior patterns and attitudes that would have turned her off when you first met—they will *always* turn her off.

Now that you know how to judge where you stand in your relationships, and how to recognize and avoid some of the more serious problems and pitfalls which may lie ahead, you are ready to consider the long-term possibilities. . . .

8

Will It Last?

THE LONG-TERM SUCCESS of a relationship depends on the interaction of an unlimited number of variables—the majority being specific to that relationship. Many conflicts, both large and small, will arise and it takes constant, honest communication, as well as understanding, commitment, sacrifice, energy, and an enlightened attitude to work these problems out and keep moving forward. In time, your relationship may follow one of several paths, depending on how successfully you handle this complicated process of maintenance and growth.

Does She Want to See Other People?

Sometimes the problems in a relationship will go unnoticed until they have reached the point where they threaten its very existence. At this point, you may wonder, "What happened? . . . Everything was so perfect." But everything wasn't perfect—a relationship rarely disintegrates overnight, and if it appears as though it has, it is only because you have ignored the many symptoms which indicated that problems were developing. In order to maximize your chances of maintaining a successful relationship, it is important to become more familiar with these many warning signs, and the following list is provided for this purpose. Read and re-read the list carefully—your ability to recognize these symptoms in their infancy can prevent unnecessary disaster.

40 SYMPTOMS OF A TROUBLED RELATIONSHIP

1. After seeing her for a considerable length of time, you still have absolutely no idea where you stand in the relationship. She never says anything to let you know, and her actions—often being contradictory—only confuse you further. As time passes, you feel more and more helpless and insecure, sensing that the fate of the relationship is entirely in her hands.

2. The relationship feels terribly one-sided. You are always phoning *her*, you are always asking *her* out, you are the one who always makes the plans, you are the one who always initiates sex, etc. But you let things continue in this fashion because deep down, you feel that the relationship would come to a dead halt if you stopped giving 200 percent to make it work.

3. She constantly talks about the virtues of a healthy progressive open relationship, and she is always encouraging you to see other women. You, on the other hand, have no desire to see any other women, and would be devastated if she was seeing other men.

4. Sometimes you get the feeling that she goes out with you only when she has no one else to be with and nothing better to do. Although she plays a central part in your life, you feel like a stand-in in hers.

5. Every time you try to discuss where the relationship is going, she tells you that she doesn't want to have any heavy discussions. If you press her, she tells you that you are taking the relationship too seriously. "Can't you just enjoy the relationship without having to analyze it?" she may ask. She seems to view the relationship far more casually than you do, and she doesn't appear to care very much whether or not you will still be seeing each other five years, five months, or even five weeks from now.

6. Although she does not criticize you directly, she is terribly critical of other people who have the same attitudes or behavior patterns you have. It doesn't take long for you to figure out that her disparaging remarks are a thinly veiled attack on you.

7. Whenever she seems hurt, angry, or upset, your first concern is to find out what is wrong and to try to make her feel better. When you are hurt, angry, or upset, she seems not to notice, and you often sense that her disregard is intentional.

8. You don't have much fun when you are with her.

Laughter is infrequent, and often feels forced. This is particularly bothersome because you know that when you are with other friends, you enjoy yourself a lot more. Clearly, there is something unhealthy about the way the two of you are interacting.

9. There is no spontaneity in the relationship—you carefully plan every day and every telephone call. Even when you have a strong desire to speak to her or see her, you often resist, fearing that not enough time has passed since the last time you saw or spoke to her.

10. You are jealous and suspicious of every man she is friendly with. Whenever you see her talking to another man, or hear that she has been with another man, you become terribly insecure. You may even act in a hostile, immature fashion that is totally out of character for you, making negative (if not downright vicious) remarks about the man which are neither fair, nor accurate. Usually you do not feel better until she has thoroughly convinced you that she does not have one iota of interest in the man, and sometimes you remain suspicious regardless of how convincing her denial is. Obviously, there is no longer any trust in the relationship.

11. Her behavior is totally unpredictable. One day she may be so cold and aloof that you expect her to end the relationship at any moment—the next time you see her, she is bubbly and affectionate, acting as though the two of you are together on top of the world. Her behavior is unsettling, and you can't help but feel that regardless of how

positive things are on her good days, the relationship is heading for disaster.

12. You constantly feel the need to prove yourself to her—you talk a lot about your positive qualities, you exaggerate your accomplishments, etc. Obviously, you don't think she values the relationship as much as you do, and you are trying to give her reasons why she should.

13. You are elated by every little bit of positive reinforcement she gives you, and you are constantly searching for anything which can be interpreted as such. You are also destroyed by every indication, however small, that the relationship may be in jeopardy. You are so hypersensitive to her words and actions that your emotional state on any given day has become completely dependent upon what she says or does on that day.

14. She is not at all receptive to your sexual needs and moods. Instead, she only sleeps with you when *she* is in the mood—which isn't very often. If she is not in the mood, and you try to change her mind, she either freezes you out or gets angry at you, making you feel as though you have done something wrong.

15. Whenever the two of you have an argument, you are always the one to apologize, even if you are convinced that she is 100 percent in the wrong. Her unwillingness to apologize makes you suspect that if you didn't take the blame, she would use the argument as an excuse to break off the relationship.

16. You will do anything to keep the relationship alive.

You tolerate whatever she says and does, no matter how abusive it is, because you are afraid of making any waves.

17. Every time you are with her you feel as though it could easily be the last. As a result, you are constantly devising clever schemes which will insure you another opportunity to be with her (you may, for example, buy a pair of tickets to a concert given by her favorite performer, knowing that she would find it extremely difficult to turn down such an opportunity). As she becomes more distant, your plans may become even more elaborate (you may, for example, offer to take her on a trip to an exotic vacation spot, or you may fake an injury or illness just to make her visit you at home).

18. She is constantly "space-talking"—talking about how important it is for a person to have plenty of his or her own space, talking about her fear of being smothered in a relationship, talking about how crucial it is for her to maintain her independence, etc. Although she often discusses her feelings in vague, abstract terms, her obsession with the topic makes you suspect that she is trying to subtly push you away.

19. You are constantly looking to others for advice and information, discussing the relationship with anyone who is willing to lend an ear. The only person you can't talk to about the relationship is the person you want to talk to most: her.

20. You have difficulty sleeping, spending hours awake in bed analyzing and reanalyzing the relationship until you

have convinced yourself that things are not as bad as they seem.

21. The two of you get along much better when you are apart than when you are together. She is always pleasant, charming, and encouraging when you speak on the telephone, but when you get together she is difficult and argumentative.

22. You remember every little thing she tells you—all of her likes, dislikes, interests—no matter how insignificant. She, on the other hand, never seems to remember the things you tell her—not even the very important things. As a result, you find yourself telling her the same things over and over again. Although you would like to think that her forgetfulness stems from a bad memory orinability to concentrate, you know that it is far more likely that it stems from a lack of interest.

23. Unable to communicate honestly with her, you manipulate her close friends by developing friendships with them in order to use them as sources of information and advice. Often, you deliberately talk to them about the relationship in mock confidence, knowing that they will tell her everything you said.

24. You are constantly making sacrifices to keep the relationship alive—she sacrifices nothing. The entire relationship seems to be operating at her convenience, and you sense that she wouldn't have it any other way.

25. She periodically complains that the relationship is smothering her, and she uses this excuse to justify spending less and less time with you.

26. She is all you ever think about, and the worse the relationship gets, the more your obsession grows. You are constantly worrying about exactly what you will say to her the next time you see her, and what you can do to stop her from ending the relationship. Your inability to concentrate on anything else is taking its toll on your work and on your other friendships.

27. She often says things which seem to be deliberately intended to hurt you or turn you off (she may tell you that she has never met a man she could live with, that serious involvements are too much of an emotional drain, that she doesn't think she is capable of giving herself fully in a relationship, or that she is at a point in her life where she just wants to go out and have a good time).

28. You are never really comfortable around her—never able to relax and be yourself. Whenever you are with her, you behave differently than you do with any of your other woman friends, acting in a way which you think she would find more attractive. If you slip, and let a little bit of the real you show, you find yourself apologizing or offering an explanation for your actions.

29. She often tells you that you would be happier with a different type of woman. When she says this, you sense she is really thinking that *she* would be happier with a different type of man.

30. She takes small, seemingly insignificant spats and blows them up into full-scale, relationship-threatening fights. You get the feeling that she is trying her hardest to create an excuse to end the relationship.

31. Whenever her telephone is busy for an extended period of time, you are suspicious that she is talking to another man. When you finally reach her, you manipulate the conversation in an effort to make her reveal who she was speaking to. If she is away from her home for an entire evening, you are beside yourself—your mind runs wild trying to figure out where she could be, and whether or not she is out with another man. When you finally do speak to her, you press her for information, and you are not satisfied until you find out exactly where she was and who she was with. Instead of reassuring you that you have nothing to worry about, she berates you for being insecure.

32. If you stop calling her for a while, she doesn't call you to find out why. Instead, she just waits for you to eventually call. Sometimes you get the feeling that if you didn't call her for a year, she wouldn't even call you to ask why (and that you might even be doing her a favor). Clearly, the relationship is a lot more important to you than it is to her.

33. It feels as though you spend more time analyzing the relationship than you do relating—your conversations are almost always very serious and analytical, and often very negative. None of your other friendships are like this.

34. You make a big production out of events such as her birthday, Valentine's Day, and Christmas, buying her special gifts or making elaborate plans that entail weeks, or even months, of preparation. She rarely seems to be as grateful as you expect her to be, and she never reciprocates; quite the contrary, she often forgets about your birthday,

Valentine's Day, and other times that are important to you.

35. If you are at her home when another man telephones, she does not tell him that she cannot speak because she has company, but instead, acts as though she is home alone. Sometimes she stays on the telephone for fifteen minutes or more; she may even go into another room to talk, leaving you to sit by yourself and fume the entire time. She may do this even if the two of you are in bed together when the phone rings.

36. When you sleep with her, you usually feel as though you are just having sex, not making love. She doesn't contribute much to your lovemaking, and often seems to be going through the motions as a matter of duty. This gives you the distinct impression that she neither wants to sleep with you nor enjoys sleeping with you, but if you question her, she tells you that you are just oversensitive.

37. Whether she has a serious problem or needs a small favor, you are always willing to go out of your way to help her. She, on the other hand, never seems to be there when you need her.

38. She cancels her plans with you on a regular basis, and sometimes completely forgets that you even had plans to see each other. You, on the other hand, go out of your way to avoid canceling any plans you have to see her, even if it means neglecting more important obligations. Your inability to cancel plans does not stem from a fear of disappointing her, or from an overwhelming need to be with her—it stems from a fear that she will be happy that you

canceled and that she will be difficult to pin down again.

39. Even if she does something that hurts you or offends you, she won't admit she is wrong. Instead, she says you would not have been hurt if you weren't so oversensitive and didn't take the relationship so seriously.

40. You're afraid to tell her how you feel about her because deep down you are almost certain that she doesn't feel the same way about you. If you *do* tell her, she does not seem happy to hear it—certainly not as happy as you would be to hear the same thing from her. She may even tell you that you are taking the relationship too seriously, and that perhaps it might be a good idea to cool things down for a while. If she says this, you immediately try to play down what you said, insisting that it sounds more serious than it really is.

Now that you are more familiar with these warning signs, you should find it much easier to spot them when they first surface in their less-severe forms. But what do you do once you notice them?

Ease off immediately.

The first thing to do is take some pressure off the woman. Give her more breathing room and some time to herself—she needs it. Trying to move closer to her will only aggravate the situation (unless, of course, her major complaint is that you are too aloof).

Give in to her needs.

Pay close attention to what she says or intimates she needs, and give it to her, even if she tells you that the two of you should stop spending so much time together or that she thinks it would be a good idea to see other people. If she *does* start seeing other people, you should too—the last thing you want to do is sit home alone and pine. Whatever you do, don't argue with her. A woman often voices such needs when she feels the relationship is smothering her—your refusal to comply with her requests will only convince her that she is right.

Go back to basics.

Many of the above symptoms indicate that certain necessary prerequisites for a strong relationship are lacking in yours; namely, communication, trust, and solid friendship. If you want the relationship to move forward, you must first establish (or reestablish) and strengthen these elements, even if it feels as though you are taking a few steps backward.

Learn from your mistakes.

If and when things do improve, don't return to the same old behavior patterns that jeopardized your relationship the first time (hopefully, with the help of her input and your improved judgment, you will know what you did wrong). If you want the relationship to survive, you must make your changes *permanent*.

Is It Too Late?

Suppose you don't notice the symptoms of your troubled relationship until they are full-blown—is there anything you can do once the relationship has come apart? I'm often asked this question by the men in my seminars (usually, at the end of my three-hour discussion)—realizing all of the things they wouldn't do if they had a chance to do it all over again, they want to know if they can get that second chance.

The answer to this depends a great deal on the woman. For some women, done is done, and they make it a habit not to look back on previous bad relationships—especially if they feel certain that the problems which led to the breakup are irreconcilable. But many women are not as inclined to flush all the memories of past relationships out of their minds, and as time passes, the positive feelings they had toward you—those which were pushed into the recesses of their minds by all the negative feelings—slowly resurface. But this process takes a *long* time—at least many months, if not longer. How can you encourage this? By simply leaving her alone for a while. This doesn't mean that you must make believe you disappeared off the edge of the universe (though it couldn't hurt)—a rare phone call or two to say hello is acceptable—but you shouldn't call very often, and you should *never* press her to go out with you. Any premature attempt to put yourself back in the mainstream of her life will only hurt any chance you have of getting her back—you must have an inordinate amount of patience.

In time, the woman's feelings may slowly start to change. At this point, she will seek you out—she may call you, or even ask to see you for old times' sake. Should this happen, it is important that you handle this opportunity properly, especially since it may only come once. This means that you cannot afford to interpret her interest as an open invitation to rush back into the relationship and make everything the way it used to be—it rarely is. Instead, you must treat the relationship as though it were brand new. This means that *you must reestablish your friendship before you even consider doing anything else.* This will also take time—probably more time than it would take in a brand-new relationship—but you must continue to be patient.

After a while, you will be able to sense whether or not the woman seems interested in developing something more than a friendship. But this must be more her decision than yours, and it cannot be forced. If she does decide to give the relationship a second chance, you can *never* let yourself fall back into your old behavior patterns. She is giving you this chance because she is convinced you have changed; one bad slip and she will conclude that it's still the same old you—the you she wanted no part of.

Looking toward the Future

Let's now suppose that your relationship has weathered the major and minor crises, and seems to be slowly, steadily growing. What happens next? Although it is possible for a relationship to continue on for years with nothing more than an understanding of commitment, most people usually are not satisfied with such a loose arrangement, and in time, tend to look for a more tangible manifestation of their commitment:

LIVING TOGETHER — IS IT THE ANSWER?

One popular choice of many couples today is the so-called living-together arrangement (sometimes referred to as a trial marriage)—an arrangement which supposedly provides most of the benefits of marriage without all of the legal and psychological restrictions. But the relative success of such an arrangement is strongly dependent upon what a couple expects to gain from it.

There are some people who are content viewing living together as an end in itself—an alternative lifestyle which provides many comforts one cannot have living alone. For these people—whether they are looking for companionship, a stronger statement of commitment, or someone to help pay the rent—living together may yield its greatest benefits, especially since their expectations are relatively modest.

But what about the many men and women who enter into a living-together arrangement to test their marital compatibility? People who live together for this reason are those who are most likely to be disappointed, for although such an arrangement will discourage many couples from tying the knot, it offers no guarantees for those who are not discouraged. In fact, most studies indicate there is no appreciable difference between the divorce rate of couples who have lived together before marriage and the divorce rate of those who have not.

Certainly one would expect to find that living together helps at least a little bit more than the statistics would indicate, but there are several reasons why it seems not to:

Best-behavior syndrome.

When two people live together to test their marital compatibility, they often approach such an arrangement on their absolute best behavior—especially in the beginning. But with everyone trying so hard to make things work, it can take a long time—perhaps years—before two people discover just how compatible they really are (this takes a long time even when two people *aren't* on their best behavior). This implies that a *brief* trial marriage can be terribly deceptive.

Many couples find this out the hard way. Often, after living together for only a few months, they decide to get married; one year later, when problems begin to surface, each wonders, "Why didn't I see this when we were living together?" Why? . . . Because they didn't live together long enough to give themselves the chance (among other reasons).

Even if a couple lives together for a long time, it is still not always an honest test of marital compatibility. This is because there is a big difference between being together fifteen months and being together for fifteen years (or fifty)

—especially with all of the stresses marriage brings (the complications of children, in-laws, financial hardships, etc.).

Bailing-out syndrome.

Living together does not require nearly the same degree of psychological commitment that marriage requires, and many people are drawn to a trial marriage for this very reason—after all, if they don't like it, they can always bail out (although one can also bail out of a marriage, it is a far more complicated process). Yet because people tend to get along much better when they know they are not strapped-in to a relationship, this bailing-out option—by taking a lot of the pressure and burden of commitment out of a relationship—creates an artificial state of bliss. It is this artificial state which often collapses soon after a couple has taken their vows.

MARRIAGE: OUT OF THE FRYING PAN . . .

Perhaps the most popular way for a couple to show their commitment to each other is through the age-old institution of marriage. But this arrangement also offers no guarantees, as the current divorce rate so clearly illustrates. It is not my intention to put marriage down, I only wish to offer one last word of advice: if you and your bride-to-be are not both 100 percent committed to making your marriage work, make sure you put this book away in a safe place—you never know when you may need it again.

9

Of Special Interest

How Aggressive *Is* the "Aggressive New Woman"?

WITH WOMEN becoming far more aggressive in the world of business, one would naturally expect this new attitude to extend into their private lives as well. To some extent, it has—women *have* become much more aggressive *inside* the bedroom. But to a larger extent, it has not, for the majority of women still find themselves trapped in very traditional, nonaggressive roles when it comes to meeting and going out with men.

DO WOMEN EVER PICK-UP MEN?

Although today's women are less prone to playing coy, and more prone to making themselves easily approachable (encouraging a man's interest through the use of eye contact, smiling, and other body language), if you're waiting for a woman to walk up to you from out of the blue and try to pick you up, you will probably be waiting a very long time. Why haven't women become that much more aggressive? Several possibilities have been suggested:

- Women are afraid of having their aggressive attitudes misread as a sexual come-on.
- Women are afraid of facing rejection, and thus protect their egos by hiding behind traditional roles.
- Women have difficulty overcoming deeply ingrained behavior patterns, and feel awkward playing a role that is traditionally a masculine one.

But whatever their reasons are, this implies only one thing for you: if you want to meet a woman, you must still be prepared to play the traditional role of the initiator or aggressor.

DO WOMEN EVER ASK MEN OUT?

What happens once you have met a woman—can you expect her to become more aggressive after the initial awkwardness of the first meeting has passed? Although various television commercials may have you convinced that a gorgeous blonde will be calling you at any moment to ask you to come to her place for a few drinks, most studies tell us otherwise. In fact, current research suggests that women's inability to change from being pursued to being the pursuer continues on long after the first meeting—most women have a lot of difficulty picking up the phone.

What is most interesting is the attitude younger women have toward asking men out. One might expect that a woman who grew up in the midst of the Women's Liberation Movement would not find it difficult to call a man on the telephone and ask him out—certainly not as difficult as an older woman would find it (a woman who has so many deeply rooted behavior patterns and attitudes to overcome). But a recent study of college students at the University of Arizona suggests this is just not so. In this study, female students were given the name of a male student to call, and the same male students were given the names of these women. The students were then instructed to contact each other within one week, but they were also told that only one of the two people should make the call (although they didn't specify *which* one). In over 90 percent of the cases, the men wound up calling the women.*

As this, and other studies indicate, the burden of playing the role of the aggressor—and all of the anxiety associated with this role—still rests predominantly on men's shoulders, in spite of Women's Lib.

* *The New York Times*, April 28, 1981; III, 1:5.

Office Romance: What Are the Risks?

As women enter the work force in ever-increasing numbers, the workplace is providing men with some of their best opportunities to meet single women. But this forces me to recall the old proverb about the intelligent pooch who refrains from doing certain unsanitary things in his own backyard (if you don't remember the proverb, use your imagination). What I'm trying to tell you is that before you entangle yourself in a steamy affair with the woman who melted your heart the first time you bumped into her in the Xerox room, you had better stop and evaluate the situation rationally: when it comes to office romance, you've got to know where to draw the line.

IS SHE "SAFE?"

It is a fact of life that the more a man and a woman work together, the more prone they are to developing a more-than-businesslike interest in each other. But it is also a fact of life that in the business environment, the closer the working relationship is, the more dangerous it is to have any romantic entanglements. In other words, although it is easiest to develop an attraction to the women with whom you have a primary working relationship (your secretary, your partner, or your boss), these are the women whom you should be trying your hardest to avoid (romantically, that is). There are several reasons for this:

• Many business executives argue that office romances are usually counterproductive. This opinion receives strong support from a recent study done at the State University of New York at Albany, which showed that there was a negative effect on job performance and productivity in 90 percent of the office romances they studied.* In light of these findings, your job, and hers, could be in jeopardy from the moment your higher-ups get wind of your amorous adventures (and the way office gossip is, sooner or later they *will* find out).

• There is the problem of the messy ending. Although your romance may eventually come to an end, there is no guarantee that your business relationship will end at the same time. Therefore, until you quit, she quits, or you both get fired, the two of you will still have to work with each other just as closely as you did when the relationship was hot and heavy. This could be a terrible emotional strain for both of you.

As I said earlier, there will be plenty of women coming in and out of your office building who don't have such a close working relationship with you. If you are wise, you will keep an eye out for these women, while maintaining your professionalism when you are in your own backyard. Needless to say, always be discreet—holding hands in the employees' cafeteria or sending love notes through the word

**The New York Times*, April 17, 1982; II, 10:1.

processor can lead to the kind of office chatter you can live very nicely without.

Who Picks Up the Tab?

It is worth taking a moment to address a question which is becoming increasingly controversial: who pays the bill? Opinions on this sensitive issue are mixed. Some women vehemently insist on paying their own way, while others are instantly turned off by men who ask them for money; some traditional men feel that a man should always pay, while other liberated men firmly believe that a woman should always take care of her share. Who is right?

Until the rules of etiquette are officially rewritten, it is difficult to say if anyone is wrong or right—but that doesn't help you very much when the bill comes to your table. Since most problems arise when the tab gets steep (splitting a bill for five dollars is no big deal, splitting a bill for seventy-five dollars is another story), your new low-key approach will enable you to avoid many of the financial complications brought on by wining and dining; but there will still be small bills which must be paid. How should they be handled?

The most important thing to do is make sure the issue of paying the bill doesn't create any problems. Getting along with the new woman is hard enough—the last thing you want to do is give yourself more trouble, especially unnecessary trouble. The following guidelines will help:

SUGGESTED PAYING ETIQUETTE

If you asked her out. If you arranged the get-together, it is recommended that you do the following:

1. Always be *prepared* to pay for the two of you—after all, it was you who did the inviting.

2. Never grab the check and pay it without giving a woman the opportunity to voice her desire to share the cost—many women feel it is very important to pay for their share, and will be angered if you don't give them the chance to do so. The best way to give a woman this chance is *not* by holding a discussion on how the bill is to be paid—this will only embarrass her into paying (one strike against you). Instead, just let the bill sit on the table for a few minutes before attempting to pay it—this subtle gesture will let her know you are open to suggestion, and will also give her the opportunity to make an offer.

3. If a woman wants to pay for her share, accept her money without an argument. Failure to do so can infuriate her.

4. If a woman offers to pay her share, but seems hesitant, it is best to either:

- Thank her for her offer, but tell her that it isn't necessary (especially if you can afford to pay the bill a lot more easily than she can).

or

- Thank her for her offer, and tell her she can leave the tip if she would like, or she can buy dessert later on, etc. (especially in situations where you could use some help, but you still know you can afford to spend much more than she can).

or

• Tell her that this time it's your treat, but you'll let her treat you the next time (especially if you know she can easily afford to). This way, your generous gesture has avoided making her feel awkward, but at the same time, you have let her know that you don't plan to pay all of the future bills.

5. Never *insist* that a woman pays for her share ("Okay . . . you owe me twelve dollars and eighty-seven cents")—this is a good way to make sure she will never want to see you again. If you want a woman to help you share the expenses of going out and she doesn't make any offer to do so (yet you know she can easily afford to), it is best to be a sport the first time you are with her and say something such as, "This one is on me—I'll let you treat the next time." As I said just before, this gesture avoids putting a woman on the spot, but at the same time, it lets her know that if she wants to continue to go out with you, she's going to have to be willing to help you out.

6. If you know you will be splitting the bill, keep this in mind when you make the plans—nothing angers a woman more than a man who suggests a restaurant or some other activity without any regard for a woman's budget.

If she asked you out. During that rare occasion when a woman asks you out:

1. The woman will almost certainly be prepared to pay for herself, and perhaps, for the both of you. Since the former is more likely than the latter (most women feel it is perfectly reasonable to go dutch under these circumstances), you should be ready to pay for your share and offer it without hesitation. If you are unwilling to pay your own way, don't accept her invitation.

2. If it looks as though you're going to get stuck for the entire tab, it is usually best to swallow your pride, pay the bill, and accept it as a learning experience—now you know something about the woman that you didn't know before. Demanding that she pay will only insure that you never see her again (of course, if this is all right with you, then do whatever makes you happy).

Although the suggested paying etiquette above addresses the problems incurred when paying for a bill in a restaurant, the principles behind these suggestions can be applied to paying for any type of expense (movie tickets, tennis court time, etc.). Again, the most important thing to remember is that you don't want the issue of paying for these expenses to create any unnecessary problems. This means that *you must be flexible* in every situation.

Herpes Etiquette

For many men and women today, the greatest fear about starting a new relationship is not the fear of rejection, nor is it the fear of sexual pressure—it is the fear of herpes. With one wave of the hand, the current herpes epidemic has sent people all over the country running for cover. For the celibate and the monogamous, herpes has become the watchword of their faith; for the incurably sexually active, it has become a reason to envy the celibate and monogamous.

At the present time, over 20 million Americans have genital herpes, and their ranks are growing. This, of course, leads to many troublesome questions for those who are considering tempting fate: how do you spot herpes? Is there any polite way to ask a woman whether or not she has an infection? If you have it, how soon should you let a woman know? Or should you keep it to yourself? During my "FOR MEN ONLY" seminars, these were often the first questions I was asked—although herpes is not in everyone's system, it is clearly on everyone's mind.

As many of us know, herpes can be difficult to detect—even with a very good flashlight—especially since the obvious symptoms all but disappear whenever the disease is in remission. So how do you find out whether or not someone has it? Well, if a woman doesn't seem willing to volunteer the information, sooner or later, you will probably want to ask. But this still provides no guarantees, since:

- Not all women are willing to be so honest, especially women who view you as nothing more than a casual fling; honesty comes with commitment.
- Honesty is not always sufficient. Much evidence sug-

gests that carriers—people who have the virus in their systems, but are unaware of its presence because they have never suffered from an outbreak—can still pass the virus on to you.

In light of this discouraging information, what can be done about herpes? At the moment, not much—but we can learn to look at it in a more positive framework. For although herpes has shaken up the entire nation, it is already responsible for some very positive changes in social behavior:

- Herpes has dealt a crippling blow to the one-night stand, giving people the long-awaited excuse they needed to turn away from the promiscuity that characterized the 60s and 70s. It is now widely believed that even if a cure for herpes comes along, the one-night stand will never again enjoy the popularity it once had.
- Because sexual contact presents certain new risks, many people are asking themselves, "With whom am I willing to take these risks?" This is encouraging men to look upon sexual intimacy as something to be shared only with women they consider special.
- Men are making more of an effort to establish honest communication prior to sexual intimacy. Although this honest communication is initially being used by men as a means of determining whether or not they risk infection, it also serves as a basis for relationship growth.

What about those men who already suffer from herpes—should they let their partners know? Although there is much debate about this, I feel it is only fair to be honest. This doesn't mean that you have to tell a woman about your infection the first day you meet her, but it does mean that you should tell her *before* you ever sleep with her. Although there is no denying that this will scare some women off, if a woman cares enough about you, she will accept the risk—one woman like this is worth a dozen who don't care enough.

The Lure of "Younger Women"

Our society is obsessed with youth. Millions upon millions of dollars are spent every year on products and surgical procedures which make people look and feel younger, while teenage starlets are the focus of all our attention. It is no wonder that in a society such as this, men have so much difficulty resisting the temptation of getting involved with attractive, nubile, younger women.

But today's women are enough of a challenge without throwing in an additional complicating factor—and believe me, age is a very big complicating factor. There is a tremendous difference between sexual maturity and emotional maturity; younger women rarely know what they want from their relationships, and they can drive a man crazy in the process of trying to find out. In fact, a relationship with a younger woman isn't really apt to be much of a relationship at all, but instead, something more closely resembling a roller-coaster ride in which your emotions are strapped to the seat. Indeed, you will be hard-pressed to find any man who has emerged from such a relationship without a badly shaken sense of self-esteem.

If you take your relationships seriously, and you hope to establish something meaningful between yourself and a woman, leave the younger women for the younger men—these men may not have an easier time than you would, but they usually don't have as much of a choice . . . you do!

NOTE: How "young" is a younger woman? Although age is certainly a factor, there is no mathematical formula which can tell you whether or not a woman is too young for you. It is best to think of a younger woman as any woman who is at a different stage in her life than you are, and has not yet reached your level of emotional maturity—regardless of whether she is ten years or ten days younger than you.

Some Praise for "Older Women"

With old social prejudices slowly eroding, men are finding a new type of relationship to be increasingly alluring—a relationship with a so-called older woman. Logistically, the increase in the popularity of such a relationship makes perfect sense—as more and more women pursue their careers in lieu of marriage and family plans, and as the divorce rate skyrockets, the number of available women in their thirties and forties is increasing dramatically. But what kind of men will these women be looking for?

Although many women will search for a conventional partner—an older or divorced man who is traditionally considered to be an older woman's peer—others, not needing the security that a man their age can offer, will eye the younger male population in search of a more energetic, sexually well-matched partner. Should we be wary of these women? Certainly not. Mature women usually have a much better idea of what they want and need from a man, and they aren't afraid to let you know. If you meet their needs, and they meet yours, your relationship can be far more rewarding and far less troublesome than the typical 80's relationship. Still, there are a few things you should know if you are considering getting involved with an older woman:

- An older woman *will* be somewhat sensitive to the age difference between the two of you. Don't aggravate this by making it a constant topic of conversation. In other words, don't go around putting down younger women all of the time, and don't constantly try to explain why you are so well suited for an older woman—she doesn't want to hear it. This kind of talk will make her feel *less* comfortable in the relationship, not more, because she will sense that you feel much more awkward about the age difference than she does.
- Don't even consider playing games with her. Although a less mature woman may put up with a little bit of gamesmanship, an older woman will disappear the mo-

ment she senses that you are toying with her emotions.

• Don't try to *act* a lot older than you are if you don't *feel* a lot older than you are. Just be yourself—that's what attracted her to you in the first place.

• Don't waste her time. If you are not comfortable giving of yourself honestly and openly, let her find someone who is.

Are You Ready for a Single Mother?

Due to a never-ending number of marital failures, the population of single mothers is steadily growing. As a result, it is becoming more and more likely that the average male will eventually come into contact with such a woman. But are you ready for a relationship with a single mother? Knowing what these women expect from their relationships should help you decide.

The majority of single mothers are looking for a man who can help ease the burden of single parenting. These women are not looking for a relationship that is all fun and games—they are looking for someone who is willing to make a commitment to them and to their children. If this is too much for you to handle, do not get involved—not only will you be wasting a woman's precious time, but you will also be stopping her from finding a man who can offer her what she really needs.

Some single mothers have a bitter taste in their mouths from their previous marriages. Often, these women are not looking for new marital prospects or serious commitments, but instead, want to maintain their single-parent status for a while. Although women like this demand much less from the men they go out with, they will still be insulted if you try to ignore that they have children. If you want to get involved with a woman like this, you must make certain adjustments in your behavior that account for the fact that she is a mother:

- You should occasionally try to make plans that involve her children (on a weekend afternoon, for example)—even if she doesn't think it's a good idea, she'll appreciate your consideration.
- You cannot try to keep her out all night if she says she wants to get home to her children—this will only make her think you are selfish and inconsiderate.
- If she has young children, it is unfair to expect her to pay for a baby sitter every time you go out. If you want to see her, you should be willing to help pay for the sitter (at least offer to help—if she doesn't want you to, that's her decision).

If these suggestions don't sit well with you, you'd better think twice before pursuing any single mothers.

Sometimes, especially when a relationship is just beginning, it is difficult to ascertain exactly what a woman with children expects from you. When this happens, it is best to put all of your cards on the table as soon as possible—tell her how you feel about children, marriage, etc.—then let her decide whether or not she is interested in a man who feels the way you do. This takes a lot of integrity, but it is only fair to her.

The Divorced Male: Can He Compete?

With the ever-increasing popularity of divorce, it is not uncommon for a man to hold on to his automobile for a lot longer than he can hold on to his wife. For those whose marriages turn over this quickly, reentering the "single" world isn't terribly traumatic. But a man who is exiting from a ten-year (or perhaps longer) marriage is likely to find a whole new world out there—a world whose rules are completely unfamiliar to him. As one recently divorced man told me, "When I first started dating again after my divorce, I felt like I was on another planet—women found my compliments to be insulting, my insults to be complimentary—everything had been turned upside-down." Another man admitted, "After a few dates, I ran back to my wife and begged her to give the marriage a second chance. But she wanted no part of it—she was enjoying being single again. I couldn't understand it . . . how could anyone enjoy this mess?"

Can men such as these compete in today's singles' marketplace? Only with great difficulty. So much *has* changed, that even men who have been single and socially active throughout all these changes are still constantly frustrated, confused, and disappointed. But men who have been removed from all of these changes are in a far worse position, for they have no relevant previous experience to learn from. If you are one of these men, you have two options:

Stick to your own kind.

The easy way out of the divorced man's dilemma is to restrict your social activities to women who are in the same boat you're in—older, divorced women who also missed out on the many changes in social interaction that took the country by storm over the past few decades. But these women are hard to find.

Go back to school.

A far more unpleasant, but often necessary course of action is reeducation. If you wish to positively interact with the new woman, you must first find out more about her. What turns her on? What turns her off? How should you attempt to handle your relationship? How *shouldn't* you handle them? With the help of this book and other pertinent information, you must learn about everything you have missed since you got married and turned a deaf ear to these issues. Although this is a difficult process, and you may fall flat on your face a few times (even the most experienced men often fall flat on their faces), in the long run you will be much better off.

10

In Conclusion

THE FIRST TIME I taught my "FOR MEN ONLY" seminar, one of the men came up to me at the end of the class and said, "I just wanted to thank you . . . you've made me realize that all of these years I've been my own worst enemy." It has been my intention for this book to have a similar effect on you. For once you have recognized that men's troubles with the new woman are largely a result of attitudes and social behavior patterns which are no longer appropriate, you have overcome the major obstacle standing between you and more successful relationships.

But even though you now understand why the old approach to women and relationships is the great disaster of the 80s, and even though it is now clear to you how little there is to be lost and how much there is to be gained by following a new path, one last problem remains: your mind may be more than willing to make positive changes, but your flesh may still be a bit weak. This should not discourage you—it is perfectly normal for this to happen. In fact, *most* men are apt to find that making the transformation from Mr. Wrong to Mr. Right, though it sounds fairly easy, actually requires time and work. Deeply ingrained behavior patterns and attitudes die hard, regardless of how well aware you are of their drawbacks.

Still, even if you must struggle to develop your new style of social interaction, it will be well worth the effort. For once you have the "right stuff" to approach the woman of the 80s with confidence and understanding, a whole new world of positive, rewarding relationships lies waiting for you just around the corner. Good luck!